Shin
Faces

Prayer
Handbook
Advent 2000 - 2001

Contributors
   Heather Pencavel, Lindsey Sanderson,
   Chris Warner, Leigh Jones

Editor
   Janet Lees

Editorial

It seems that some pray-ers find new ways of praying a threat rather than an adventure. I was in my early twenties when a lay preacher fifty years my senior first outlined to me what he had experienced as the exciting prospect that 'prayer changes'. We pray because we believe prayer changes: it changes us, our relationships, situations, people, our faith. Equally, prayer changes: it develops, grows, wanes, transforms. These are some of the adventures of prayer. What better activity to accompany our hopes and fears for regeneration than prayer.

Regeneration is not new. The UK has had many regeneration initiatives over the last fifty years and billions of pounds have been spent. At the time of writing there are many regeneration schemes in local communities throughout the UK in which faith communities are involved. The work of regeneration does not end with these prayers but is the context in which many communities live daily. If you are not involved in regeneration then try to find out about projects going on near you, perhaps linking with those churches that are involved. It can take a lot of sustained effort and energy to continue to work for regeneration and solidarity from others can be a source of encouragement. If you are involved then make the most of support networks, or consider starting one if necessary. It's about more than survival; it's about flourishing. Find ways of sharing your regeneration stories in words and pictures as we have tried to in this book. This year's contributors: Heather Pencavel and Chris Warner, both working in Industrial Mission, Lindsey Sanderson, Mission Enabler to the URC Synod of Scotland, and Leigh Jones, an artist from Sheffield, offer a wealth of insights on regeneration in church and society.

Regeneration continues, my term as editor of this prayer and worship resource ends with this book. My thanks to those who have sustained the work of these three years, and even made it fun. Particular thanks to Wendy Cooper, secretary of the committee, without whose support and skills there would be no prayer handbook. Prayer changes and the prayer handbook changes: your new editor is Norman Hart.

Janet Lees

Daily Prayer

Regeneration seems to evolve in a cyclical way, or so a group of us involved in regeneration in inner city Sheffield discovered as we shared our experiences. Searching for words and images to describe these has been an interesting and sustaining piece of work which we share with you here. A diagram of the cycle shows what I mean (see page 2).

As with any cycle, who's to say where it begins. Moreover, unlike previous years, there are more than seven days in the cycle. For our daily prayers this year you might like to try this pattern, which also differs slightly from previous years in having no predetermined starting day. Short prayers are provided for stages in the cycle of regeneration. These can be used with readings, prayers and activities which complement the daily theme from the other pages of this book - or from material found elsewhere by the user of course. Maybe a daily cycle of prayer is difficult to sustain for a whole year. A pray-er might begin the cycle in one part of the year and carry it on for one cycle or more and then not return to it for several days, weeks or even months. The pray-er can then re-enter the regeneration cycle at the point which seems appropriate at that time. Or a pray-er may decide that the use of a daily prayer cycle is more appropriate for them at certain times of the year, perhaps in Advent or Lent as traditional times for regular prayer, or during a retreat or holiday.

Could you believe a hyacinth lives in here, full of beauty & fragrance

What ever way you try to pray this year welcome a new opportunity to begin an adventure, rather than the tiresome business of putting on a worn out sock.

Regeneration cycle

void/meaninglessness/empty

learned helplessness/powerlessness/worn down

agony/betrayal/excluded

rebellion/resistance/outrage

co-operation/courage/crucible

build up/restore/regenerate

fullness/abundance/productivity

competition/individualism/self satisfaction

apathy/decline/dying

Short Prayers for Regeneration

void/meaninglessness/empty

All Knowing Nothing, All Being No-one,
how can you really be there;
hold the universe in your embrace?
I can't even shout or rage in this vacuum,
such is my emptiness.
Take it: it's all I have.
Then everything will have been given over.
I don't know anymore if I even remain?

learned helplessness/powerlessness/worn down

Look at these elbows: scuffed.
Look at these cuffs: frayed.
Look at these hands: empty.
Look at this life: powerless.
I am worn down and worn out,
unable to believe that you might have been there too.
Show me the elbows, the cuffs, the hands, the life.

agony/betrayal/exclusion

Left out again.
Still on the edge.
Ignored, excluded, abandoned
as if naked and totally vulnerable.
I fling my arms out in despair, (do this now)
my chest heaving.
As I do, maybe I'll catch a glimpse
of your mirror image.

rebellion/resistance/outrage

At least I can be angry:
keep me company, furious Creator.
At least I can dissent:
keep me company, protesting Christ.
At least I can rebel:
keep me company, revolutionary Spirit.
Holy Three, in your outrageous company,
may my resistance be tempered like steel.

co-operation/courage/crucible

Persistent God, thankfully
the signs of life are all around me,
contributing to my growth and well-being.
Now I am being lifted up.
Whatever the waste land, there's always something growing.
Like a scrawny shrub I cling to God, the Rock,
and will not be shaken.

build up/restore/regenerate

Beyond the scratched surface we seek restoration.
In the wasteland we hope for the rebuilding of community.
Healing Spirit, we recognise that we do not require the quick fix,
but the sustaining flow of vision and energy
that comes from the Holy One and makes for wholeness.

fullness/abundance/productivity

Now the river flows and the reservoir brims over.
Now the order book is full and the company thrives.
Now confidence grows and personality flourishes.
Now, Creator, we experience your energy at full strength
and we play happily as it showers on us.

competition/individualism/self satisfaction

Another yawn stifled:
Great God, are you bored too?
Another day over:
Timeless One, do you not count them?
I seem to think I've made it;
fulfilled all my potential,
with no more challenges to meet
this side of whenever.
If you are today, yesterday and forever
help me to see there's more
to life before death
than that with which I'm satisfied.

apathy/decline/dying

Going down, down, down:
whether sliding off or bottoming out,
it seems to be all downhill from here.
You, who also went down beyond life and back again,
be present in the absence,
be attentive in the apathy,
be watchful in the indifference,
keep the death vigil with me
until we rise again.

Janet Lees

Read: Jeremiah 33:14-15

God says
We're opening a new Branch
a new Partnership with people.
Israel and Judah will benefit
(it's in the terms of the contract)
Safe cities, peaceful communities
the new Branch will see to it.
Its mission will be based on just dealing
(just like the Parent company but
with a local focus)
and in time
everyone will know that this new Branch
expresses and shares the Name of God
"the LORD our Righteousness".

God of all creative enterprise
wherever companies and communities
are planning new ventures in partnership,
let the longing for justice drive their negotiations
and peace and safety be their prime concerns.
Help us and them to see
in their meetings and papers
their setbacks and achievements
the coming of God our Righteousness
whose love and justice
have always been
will always be
written into your covenant agreement
with humankind.

During the Sundays of Advent many churches light Advent candles: one candle for each of the four Sundays and one on Christmas Day, to announce the coming of Jesus, the Expected One. You will find words to accompany the lighting of Advent Candles on the right hand pages for Advent and Christmas Day. Each week follows a similar pattern: a response for everyone to say is followed by names which can be called out from within the congregation. After the candle/s are lit there is an activity to mark our recognition of people of our time who announce Christ to us, followed by a reflection on the lives and experiences of people working at Sheffield Forgemasters, a steel engineering company in Sheffield, to help you identify 'God with us' in the people around you.

We light this candle to remember the Patriarchs.

Abraham & Sarah ... Isaac & Rebecca ... Jacob & Rachel ... Joseph

Here is a people that God is making -
calls them to follow, not knowing where.
Nomads and statesmen make up the number
hearing God's call
believing God's truth:
they learn as they follow God's way to prepare.

You could hang decorated tags bearing the names of your forebears either around the advent candles or on the Christmas Tree to accompany this week's candle lighting activity.

Like the people of Israel, Sheffield Forgemasters has a long history:
- it began as a small iron and steel engineering facility in the centre of Sheffield,
- since 1864 it has operated from its River Don site where the largest steel castings and forgings in the western world are now produced,
- new and successful technical and commercial innovation are the hallmarks of the company
- the workforce is made up of highly skilled, motivated and flexible individuals

Sheffield Forgemasters Engineering was formed by the merger of River Don Castings and Forgemasters Steel and Engineering.

Heather Pencavel and Janet Lees

Pray with partner churches introducing new themes and initiatives for growth and development.

Road building is rough work
hard labour, muscles strained
hands calloused, back near breaking
even with lifting gear, hard hat, protective boots.

Site clearance is dirty work
and dangerous
removing rotten structures,
risking unsafe ground
uncovering long-forgotten corruption,
the stink too strong to breathe
of waste and dereliction

God you cry out to us
to clear the site, build the road
because you are coming
and you will come
along the road we build.

Give your people, we pray
the will and stamina for the job.
Give us courage, to tackle the clearance
of debt and exploitation
which corrupt communities and nations.
Give us the grit and determination
to straighten out the crooked structures
which make it hard for the poor and the weak
to journey to freedom.
And help us to shout aloud that you will come
along the road we build.

We light this candle to remember the prophets.

Miriam....Elijah ... Amos ... Isaiah ... Ezekiel ... Anna

Here are the Prophets God sends to the people
teaching repentance, warning of woe.
Poets and preachers speaking God's judgement,
telling God's goodness
calling for justice,
always reminding us which way to go.

You could hang decorated tags bearing the names of
contemporary prophets either around the advent candles or on the
Christmas Tree to accompany this week's candle lighting activity.

'My father worked in the casting bay' said one of the workers, now
50 years old, at Sheffield Forgemasters. '"You won't work down
the local colliery" he said to me. But times change and I see it as a
dinosaur now. Companies and industries, they have life-cycles too.
When I started at 16 all the companies in this valley were
expanding. But we're a tiny island off the mainland of Europe and
50 years from now it will all be a big Disney world with a dome
over the top to keep the weather out'.

Heather Pencavel and Janet Lees

Pray with **partner churches in the European region of CWM.**

Read: Luke 3:7-18

Hellfire preaching
uncompromising demands
straight talk – that's John,
telling it like it is.
Sometimes it all seems very simple:
God reigns, God judges
which means
just sharing of property
honest trade
no bullying, no blackmail
no greed. Simple enough.
If only ...

God you are coming to your people
to reign with justice.
Help us to recognise your coming
in fair trade campaigns
in consultations between management and workers;
in power structures which put human wellbeing
as their first priority.

Reigning, judging God,
come today to our world of trade
and show us how to make it fair;
come to our industry and work through us
to create fulfilling work and fair conditions;
come to our authority structures
and show us how to blend mercy with justice.
Let your reign of justice begin today.

We light this candle to remember John the Baptist.

John preached in the desert, "Repent, for the kingdom of heaven is close at hand."

Here's the forerunner, preaching repentance,
showing his hearers new ways to behave.
Prophet and mystic, he looks for God's kingdom,
teaching, baptising,
calling for holiness,
seeking the One who is coming to save.

You could hang decorated tags bearing the names of those who call us to repentance either around the advent candles or on the Christmas Tree to accompany this week's candle lighting activity.

'In good times, when they had money oozing out of the seams they didn't give us owt. Now it's lean times and they still wants us to tighten our belts. I say, it's time to say enough. We're the ones making the profits for this company and we deserve a fair share'.

Heather Pencavel and Janet Lees

Pray with those who work for workers' rights.

Read: Luke 1:39-56

Mary ran away - hurried off to the country to her cousin. For the last few weeks she had been coming to terms with the message - and with the physical effects of early pregnancy, as well as the fear for the future, once everyone knew her situation. Her visit to Elizabeth was a kind of escape: from the watchful eyes, soon no doubt the wagging tongues, of the villagers in Nazareth; perhaps from the reaction of her family (did they believe in angels?).
Perhaps Elizabeth - too old to join the young mothers of her village, wife of the priest set apart from the ordinary people - needed a companion, someone with whom to share her new experience, talk about the present and the future. Her young pregnant cousin was literally a Godsend.

Unexpected God
we pray for women who have to cope
with unplanned pregnancy:
for young girls whose schooling is disrupted,
lives changed for ever, families angry or disappointed;
for women who can't afford another child;
women long past hope who have to adjust
to the physical changes and emotional upheaval
of "a baby at my time of life".

Unsettling God
Thank you for women like Elizabeth
who recognise the presence of love and goodness
in the most unlikely situation,
who understand that God is born
in the coming child
and know the potential greatness
of the new life.

Show us all how to nurture your life in every child
and to make a world where everyone is welcome.

We light this candle to remember Mary.

Mary said, "You see before you the Lord's servant, let it happen to me as you have said."

Here is the mother who heard from an angel.
Amazed but obedient, she bowed to God's will.
Summoned to Bethlehem, lodged in a stable,
she cradled the baby,
saved him from Herod,
then watched as he journeyed to Calvary's hill.

You could hang decorated tags bearing the names of those you identify as contemporary 'servants of the Lord' either around the advent candles or on the Christmas Tree to accompany this week's candle lighting activity.

'She left to have a baby', they said of the woman who had worked as a Metallurgist at Sheffield Forgemasters. The workforce is largely male, though many fewer now produce the steel that is 'made in Sheffield' than did twenty years ago. 'My wife worked in the steel industry all her life' said another. She would price up the orders from large ledgers in the days before computerisation: 'My wife can tell you those prices even now'.

Heather Pencavel and Janet Lees

Pray with women in CWM; including Revd Diane Vorster, Moderator of the Uniting Presbyterian Church of Southern Africa; women's centres in Zambia, Women's Multi-racial fellowship in New Zealand; women pastors and preachers in Malaysia (for these and others see the CWM leaflet).

God
you could have come
with miracle and magic
in a flash of light
in a hurricane of judgement
so that the earth shook
and the universe trembled

but you chose to come
in a baby's newborn cry
you chose to make your coming known
to working men on a cold hillside
to wandering scholars
to an innkeeper
and to the beasts of the field

Because you came, a baby,
born to a young girl
you brought miracle and magic and mystery
into ordinary things
and the whole creation sings at your coming
and is blessed.

Isaiah 52:7-10   Psalm 98
Hebrews 1:1-4, (5-12)
John 1:1-14

We light this candle for the Christ Child.

Mary wrapped him in swaddling clothes and laid him in a manger.

Here is the baby who comes to redeem us,
milky and warm and asleep in the hay.
Knowing no danger yet, holding our future,
needing our nurture,
claiming our worship,
this king strong in weakness still governs today.

Many people work on Christmas Day. Everyone thinks, rightly of
those who work in hospitals or for the emergency services, but
there are also people working in other industries and services
today. Just as ordinary people came to the manger to see the
newborn child, so these ordinary people should be remembered in
our worship today. You could hang decorated tags bearing the
names of any you know either around the advent candles or on the
Christmas Tree to accompany this week's candle lighting activity.

'We work Christmas Day as well here you know' said one of the
workers in the furnace room. 'It's nice work if you can get it... quite
quiet, peaceful even compared with other days'. On 'other days'
some of the largest pieces of caste and forged steel being made in
the world today are heated up to 1,000 degrees centigrade and
hammered into shape by a team of workers, one of whom has to
run up to the huge molten shape at regular intervals, sweat
pouring, face shining, and measure its dimensions with a pair of
calipers to see how much more hammering needs to be done.

Heather Pencavel and Janet Lees

Pray with those who work today.

Read: Samuel 2:18-20,26 and Luke 2:41-52

*The child is missing - a moment's inattention, then
the lurch of the heart, the sinking of the stomach
"I thought he was with you"*

*The child is missing - the ache of longing, even after years
even when you know he is safe, even when there are other children,
"I wonder what he's doing now?"*

*The child is missing - wandering the streets without a home:
home is where blows are struck, and darkness brings abuse and now
"She's gone - good riddance!"*

*The child is missing - he slept last night in this shop doorway
till they came with guns, street cleansing, and he died.
"They got Carlos - tonight it might be us"*

Parent God
Hannah knew where Samuel was, and missed him.
Mary and Joseph found Jesus in the end,
safe in the Temple learning
(as well as all the teachers' knowledge)
what agony of fear his parents feel,
how much they love him.

Children disappear every day
and are not always found
though they are often missed.
We pray for all missing children and their parents:
children kidnapped and afraid,
the runaways, the disappeared,
children given for adoption.

Teach us how to build homes where everyone is valued
communities where everyone is safe
and a world where all children are able to grow
strong in mind and body
as Jesus did.

The Circular Journey

I'm nearly at the end of the first leg of my journey.
You set me down a number of years ago,
And I spent most of those years
walking away from you.
Impatient to grow up,
I walked too quickly,
travelled too far.

Where I expected fear,
I have found hope.
where I feared your absence,
I have seen your presence.
I am nearing the beginning of the second leg of my journey,
and only now do I see
that my journey is a round trip.
My goal is not to travel twice as far away,
But to reach home by nightfall.

Christina Kalvin

Pray with partner churches in the South Asia region of CWM, particularly their
work with children and young people.

Read: Isaiah 60:1-2; Matthew 2:1-8; Ephesians 3:3-10

God of the people

Where leaders rule with self-interest and greed,
oppress and eliminate their people:
there seems no hope of freedom.
We forget the secret power of stories
which reveal you as the liberator
of those who cry out in their distress.
**Give us the courage for journeying
to find where truth and justice are born.**

God of all people

When families are forced to register as consumers,
become servants of an economic god:
many get left out in the cold.
We forget the secret strength of community
to reveal the skills and contribution
of those who feel exploited and excluded.
**Make us messengers of hope
who recognise and value those society rejects.**

God with every people

While street-children are shot or put away,
innocents slaughtered in acts of ethnic cleansing:
the earth seems full of darkness.
We forget the secret skills of reflection
which reveal you at the heart
of our struggling, suffering world.
**Inspire us to search you out
and joyfully acknowledge your presence with us.**

For a New Year

Remember that Jesus
- began life as a carpenter's apprentice in his father's workshop
- was concerned about the exploitation of the poor
- recruited manual and clerical workers (and domestic workers!) to share his work
- taught us to love our neighbours
- believed in forgiving mistakes, giving second chances, making new starts
- is the unseen guest in South Yorkshire's workplaces (and every work place).

Remember that Industrial Mission
- shares Jesus' concerns for people at work or out of work
- believes that more people taking Jesus' teaching seriously would help resolve many workplace problems
- demonstrates, through its various ministries, that God *'invests in people'*.

David Halstead

Christianity is not about God's love for the Church, for good people, for religious people, for poor people. It is about God's love for the whole of humankind, the whole of creation, not just one part of it. Industrial Mission exists to remind and to reflect the depth and breadth of God's love.

Jack, Bishop of Sheffield

Pray with partner churches in the Yorkshire and Humberside region of England, and those working for regeneration.

Named and reclaimed

Redeeming God
you have called us by name.
We belong to you.

Life with you is delightful.
We know who we are because of you,
we feel safe and secure in your presence.

We have responded to you with loving obedience.
We have tried to turn heads in your direction,
to create a church where people come
to worship, learn and pray:
to gather and grow.

Yet for all our delight and determined energy,
we are aware that judgements must be made:
not by us, but of us and our ways of doing things.
Too often we claim you for ourselves,
when we should proclaim Christ - Saviour of the world.

Loving Christ, delight of our God,
rename us and reclaim us.
Turn our watery baptisms
into a fiery fulfilment
of your Spirit-filled will.

Isaiah 43:1-7   Psalm 29
Acts 8: 4-17
Luke 3:15-17, 21-22

Epiphany 1

Delight in Diversity: read Luke 3:15-17, 21-22.
A society which values diversity will be consistent and persistent in
its efforts to create greater equality. Such a society will consist of
individuals who recognise that they are more alike than they are
different. More importantly, they understand and appreciate the fact
that that which makes them different is to be valued. The challenge
for our society is to create and sustain a culture which values
human diversity and to develop institutions whose styles and
approaches are compatible with that value.

Linbert Spencer

Enjoying diversity
As the group begins its meeting invite each person to introduce
themselves by name and affirm their difference, which is then
confirmed as valuable by the group as a whole. For example:
I'm Anne, I'm different. **You are Anne, you are valuable.**
I'm Barry, I'm different. **You are Barry, you are valuable.**
If you are on your own try saying something similar aloud to
yourself as you start your prayer:
I'm Clare, I'm different, I'm valuable.

The National Family and Parenting Institute seeks to support parents
throughout the UK. One of its trustees writes:
A recent poll showed that people's top responses to being parents
were joy and pride. Most people enjoy being good parents and want
to do a good job. They also want to know what will work and how to
find help when things get tough. There are larger scale concerns
about the role of families in society, the diversity of family life, the
needs of children, what part fathers play and so on. The institute
should *listen* to parents - it's not 'experts' telling people how they
should live. It will identify what's available already, for example the
Family Caring Trust courses and the 'Homestart' scheme where
volunteers support parents as friends and share their experiences.
Parenting courses are something very practical that we can share in
now. We have the chance to move towards 'fullness of life' and to help
others do the same. My life has been changed by the experience of
parenting courses and I have seen other people's lives changed too:
that seems to me very much to do with the Christian Gospel.

David Gamble

*Pray with partner churches in New Zealand, particularly their work to support
parents and families.*

Read: Psalm 36:5-7; 1 Corinthians 12:4-11

I wish I had
the gift to turn wine into water,
magic bread, rice, beans out of the ground,
make poor people's homes strong against earthquakes
and all those personnel mines disappear!

I wish I had
miraculous powers to turn evil into good,
make hard hearted leaders really care,
take out the poverty and pain of common people,
turn military hardware into farm tools!

I wish I had
fantastic knowledge to turn sickness into health,
crack the big C, cure AIDS and HIV,
get everyone reading, writing, calculating
and creating structures and systems that serve!

I wish I had
the faith to believe that changing the world was possible,
the tongues, the prophetic voice, the ability
to translate everything into words
that everyone understood - and acted on!

God, don't you wish that your heavenly love:
your sky high faithfulness,
your mountain top righteousness,
your sea deep justice,
was found more in us?

Stick with us unfailing God:
make your wishes come true in us and through us.

Isaiah 62:1-5   Psalm 36:5-10
1 Corinthians 12:1-11
John 2:1-11

Epiphany 2

Source of Life: read John 2:1-11
The Holy Trinity is born anew in us each day of our lives. In all
making: of beds, beer and babes; in all awakening: of music,
rhyme and love; in all growing: of maize, pear and pine; in all
understanding: of ice, energy and motion; and in all mothering,
moulding and manufacturing, lies the breath of the Father.

Derek Webster

Ten old bottles

Take ten empty bottles, could be plastic or glass. On the
outside put labels which suggest some of the old things we
hope will be transformed, like the water in the story of the
wedding at Cana. These could include:

Line all the bottles up and sing this song to the tune 'Ten green
bottles', knocking the bottles off one by one;

Ten old bottles, sitting on the wall;
ten old bottles, sitting on the wall
and if one old bottle should accidently fall,
there'll be nine old bottles sitting on the wall.

Loving God, you made the difference
with a pebble in a sling,
with water at a wedding,
with a child in a manger
and by showing the Kingdom in a mustard seed.
Take our fear, our broken bodies,
our hardened hearts, our minds closed to injustice:
reshape us in your image
so we may reshape our world.

Prayer for Homelessness Sunday

Pray with **partner churches in Malawi.**

Read: Nehemiah 8:1-3, 5-6, 8-10; Luke 4:18-19

What wonderful words and so easy to understand,
good news at last:
for the poor
for prisoners
for the blind
for broken victims of every kind.
Amen to that. This is really something to celebrate:
party time!

What wise words, though quite understandable
given the situation:
scarce resources
high crime
minority interest
fragility of the free market economy.
You've got my vote. This is really a time for caution:
hang on in there!

What wrongful words so cutting, so unfair
when we do no-one any harm:
donate to charities
stay law abiding
provide access
sign petitions and write letters to our MP.
We worship every Sunday. This Word seems very harsh:
what shall we do?

Encourage us, patient God, to open the book again:
try to understand it better,
honestly face up to its challenges,
and free ourselves for service and celebration.

Nehemiah 8:1-3, 5-6, 8-10
Psalm 19   Luke 4:14-21
1 Corinthians 12:12-31a

Epiphany 3

Liberation: read Luke 4:14-21....'where he had been brought up'.

Cruddas Park is a housing estate in Newcastle upon Tyne. In the following conversation we meet an 11 year old girl who, with other local children are beginning to find a place in the local community structures, and from there into the process of urban regeneration. The concept of children being able to make their voices heard was beginning to dawn on her and, without prompting, she instigated this discussion:

Girl: Who did they ask then?

Worker: People who lived in Cruddas Park at the time.

Girl: What! All of them?

Worker: No, not all of them. They started by talking to the people who were involved in the residents' association.

Girl: What's that, residents' what, what's that then?

Worker: A group of people who get together to try to make the housing and the area a better place for people living in it ...

Girl: Well, I live here and they didn't ask me nowt!
          (the group laughs and comments that the girl would have only been little, about 5 years old at the time)

Worker: Do you think that little kids might want to say something about Cruddas Park if they live here, about the dogs and the fires?

Boy: Yeh but it'd be daft stuff, 'cause when you're a little kid you don't know ...nowt like about stuff, not proper.

Worker: What about when you get older, what about you, if they asked you now, would you think of something to say about what you liked and didn't like.

Girl: Yeh, but they wouldn't ask 'cause we're just kids.

Boy: Yeh, they should ask kids an'all, 'cause we're residents an'all... They should ask us an'all. I think I'd tell 'em!

Suzanne Speak

Coming true in a place near you?

In your group, read the discussion out loud with appropriate group members taking the parts of the girl, the boy and the development worker. Then discuss these questions together:

• in what way is the discussion about liberation?
• what do you think are the links to Jesus' experience in the synagogue in Nazareth as Luke tells it?
• how are children included in the local church or community structures where you are?
• what opinions do children have about their involvement locally?

Pray with partner churches in the North-east region of England and those working for regeneration.

25

Read: Psalm 71:1-4; 1 Corinthians 13:1-13

God our refuge and strength -
be our rock:
a craggy, cave-filled constancy,
where we can safely shelter
in the quiet solitude
of hidden places,
listening for your whispered words of wisdom
healing our loud, self-seeking love.

Be our rock:
a hilly, hope-filled hiding place,
where we can disappear,
flee from the aggression and violence
which attacks us, find refuge in the heights and depths of Love
that exceeds our hopes and expectations.

Be our rock:
a safe vantage point of vision,
where we can clearly see
the horror of destructive acts
despising love,
and speak out loud prophetic words to warn:
"faith and hope are not enough!".

Be our rock:
a high and weather torn strength,
where we can be exposed
to the rush of Your Spirit
blowing us,
blasting us with the power of creation,
holding us between fear and fascination.

Epiphany 4

Fulfilment: read Luke 4:21-30

Dreams from Hard Places

Our social history has for a long time cast a long shadow over our development. At times it has dulled our vision, eroded our confidence and reduced our communities' life blood to a mere trickle, but it is from that trickle that we must nurture the stream and let it flow more strongly until it runs, not as a stream, but as the river of our regeneration, carrying in its flow new hope, life, opportunity and economic regeneration into the heart of our communities. To achieve this we must employ all the useable vehicles at our disposal, our politics, our music, our poetry, our arts, our technology and our education but most importantly, we must employ all our own commitment to be involved. They will become the enabling implements in our hands by which we can power the change, as we seek to enter the new millennium in a strong, vibrant and inclusive society.

I came here today not as an expert of human geography, geology, social anthropology, economics or language and culture, but merely as the by-product of a particular time in the history of our people, having entered the world at a time when the language and culture of my parents was already in retreat and heading for extinction, but still I stand before you today with optimism and determination, that the passion and the spirit that has driven us to survive against all the forces of our history, is ours with which to fashion the shape of the future.

The river of our regeneration must run strong and deep and we must be the guardians of its future course. Like all great rivers it must rise from the spring nurtured from the depths but flowing outwards and enriching new lands.

Donnie Munro

Pray with partner churches in Scotland and those working for regeneration.

Read: Isaiah 6:1-8

Living God, you call out our names,
'Who will go for us?'
Here I am, send me.

We, young and old, women and men, with different gifts and skills,
people of every place and nation, speaking many languages,
sharing many life stories.

'Who will go for us?'
Here I am, send me.

Living God, we are too young, too old, too shy, too fearful
but still you send us out.
Out amongst our families and friends,
out into our communities, towns and cities,
out to live, mix and mingle with others.
You send us out with love and joy and hope
to pour cups of tea and play with children,
to listen to worried parents and deliver the church newsletter
to sign justice petitions and recycle glass bottles.

You send us out to share in your mission, wherever and whoever
we are.

Living God, you call out our names.
'Who will go for us?'
Here I am. Send me.

In 1993 Dr Sandy Logie was working at St Francis Hospital in Katete, Zambia with people who had HIV/AIDS. While there he contracted the AIDS virus from a contaminated syringe. In Zambia at least 20 per cent of the population were HIV positive at that time. When he revisited the hospital in 1999 some things had changed:

- the wards were quieter because the hospital now has to charge all its patients for treatment as a result of government efforts to meet international debt repayments, and resulting cutbacks in funding health and welfare programmes;
- the rate of infection from HIV/AIDS had risen from around 40 per cent of patients to 80 per cent and the incidence of tuberculosis has also increased.

Doctors are poorly paid in Zambia, often leaving to work in Malawi or Botswana after qualifying, where pay is better.

Christian Aid News

Pray with partner churches working with people who have HIV/AIDS, particularly in the Africa region of CWM.

Read: Luke 6:17-26

Voice 1   Holy God,
we bring to you symbols of our comfortable life;
money to pay bills, and buy things we both need and want;
food to nourish us, and overfeed our bodies;
symbols of laughter, shared amongst friends but
sometimes at the expense of others;
symbols of praise and admiration for our achievements in
life, but at what cost to others?

Holy God, we are happy being comfortable.
We enjoy your gifts.

Voice 2   But Jesus upsets our comfortable life
and challenges us to live a new way:
sharing with the poor,
not through giving what we can spare but redistributing
wealth;
feeding the hungry,
not simply at the soup kitchen, but healthy, wholesome
food for all.
mourning with the grieving,
not through well meant sympathy but through sharing in
pain, loneliness and despair,
standing up with the persecuted,
not silent support from afar, but speaking and acting for
the sake of the other.

Voice 3   Holy God, we want to be citizens of your kingdom.
Forgive us when we forget your rule of law.
Shake us up when we get comfortable and ignore the
needs of our neighbour.
Help us to get our perspectives right so your kingdom
may come.

Epiphany 6

On 21st September 1999, Taiwan was devastated by an earthquake which killed over 2,000 people and left many more thousands injured and without homes. Many people have helped in the international efforts to bring aid and regeneration to Taiwan. Here are some examples:

- the first rescue workers to reach the village of Kuoshin, where a mud flow killed 60 people and buried 40 others, had to walk four hours to get there;
- volunteers have reported mass destruction throughout the country including lost road, unsafe buildings, landslides, collapsed houses;
- within an hour of the earthquake the Changhua Christian hospital got into action; a few hours later the Presbyterian Church in Taiwan mobilised itself island wide to participate in the relief and rescue work - among their projects plans to employ 20 full time staff to serve alongside the local churches to help in the healing process and rebuilding communities;
- bodies were dug up, wounds were bandaged, tents put up and families fed and comforted but as the initial horror subsided the fears did not because thousands of aftershocks had continued;
- a young man turned up at the office of the Presbyterian Church of Taiwan: he spoke no English and it seems he had come from Japan to volunteer with the rescue work;
- CWM churches around the world sent donations for the relief work: a message from the Churches of Christ in Malawi said "Your sorrows are our sorrows, and we share the difficult situation which the church and people are in".   *CWM 'Inside Out'*

The symbols of plenty and poverty can be used to provide a visual focus in the prayer. Wads of money, plenty of food, a joke book, an educational certificate, can represent plenty. A few pennies, an empty plate, a black armband, a chain, can represent poverty.

Pray with partner churches in Taiwan, and for the rehabilitation and care centres established after the 1999 earthquake.

Our God, your love surrounds your world,
nurturing and cherishing it,
giving it life and hope.

You call us to be agents of your love,
a network of people in every place
ushering in your kingdom,
proclaiming your good news.

You ask us to share your love with the unlovely if we are to truly
follow in your way.
(pause)
We bring before you our 'enemies' today;
structures which fail to recognise God's image in each person,
promoters of a global economy at the expense of local culture and
identity,
those in our congregations who resist change and are determined
to maintain the status quo.

We bring before you the 'enemies' of our communities.
Give us eyes to see through the façade to the person inside,
and there find you.

(silence)

Our God, you ask us to love,
not to judge or condemn but bless those who curse your name,
pray for people who ill-treat us and others,
turn the other cheek when we are under attack,
willingly give when our possessions have been taken.

Epiphany 7

Love that breaks through stone

The suffering caused by war, catastrophe, natural disaster, disease is terrible, and we turn away from it in sadness and revulsion. But our liturgy calls us to account for our sins of omission as much as for sins of commission, for the things we have left undone, the good that we could but did not. Our hardness of heart extends far beyond the East Timorese and the South African AIDS sufferers to include a natural habitat that is in acute danger from western overconsumption and southern poverty, and which everywhere from inner-city Glasgow to sub-Saharan Africa includes a holocaust of destitution, marginalisation and social invisibility. Such hardheartedness demands 'a love that breaks open stone'.....

Kathy Galloway

In the cracks
It is in the cracks that the wild things grow
Bugle purpling over the stone, ox-eyes looking
Fearlessly into the sun for the light that
Will ultimately wither their sight.
Droplets of gold vetch, stretch.

She was right first time. You are the
Gardener after all, with a love that
Breaks open stone, and hands too freshly cracked
For her to touch.

Only the desperate and doubting
May press the red petaled palms
And see the pollen stain their finger tips.

Alison Swinfen

Pray with **partner churches in Nauru.**

Read: **Exodus 34:29-35; 2 Corinthians 3:12-4:2**

Voice 1   Holy God, when Moses met you on the mountain his
face shone,
reflecting your glory and power.
From that day on he was never the same.
He had encountered you and his face shone.

Loving Spirit you make our faces shine.
Help us to light up the faces of others.

Voice 2   Today you meet us on mountains and motorways,
in the home and at work, in places of great joy or despair.
We too have been changed by our encounter
and our lives will never be the same.

response

Voice 1   Holy God, when Moses returned from the mountain he
wore a veil
as the Israelites were frightened of his shining face.
Moses revealed you to his community
and from that day on they were never the same.

response

Voice 2   Today each one of us reveals who you are
in our words and actions, in our prayers and attitudes,
in our loving and hopefulness and expectation of what is
to come.
May our communities recognise you and never be the same.

response

The sunflower

All about was desolation. The stale, stinking canal, the old Victorian tenements, the streets with the rubbish of last month still piled in the gutters, the lamp-posts broken. Some of the flats were all boarded up, others had their windows broken, all, or nearly all, looked sad, tired and as if they should have been pulled down years ago. There are many places like it and worse.

At the end of Jubilee Street the desolation was complete. For thirty years a bomb site had been there... it was covered with broken pieces of masonry and the inevitable litter.. It defeated even the most vigorous and persistent of weeds. Nothing grew there until one autumn a seed took root. The following spring nobody noticed the plant for several weeks, but in the end you cannot miss a sunflower. There it stood, five or six feet tall, with its heavy, golden head. When the sun was out, its yellow was so intense that most people would shield their eyes against it but on dull days it shone, almost as powerfully as if a strange light of its owned burned within its petals.

It caused quite a stir. Most of the local people had never seen a sunflower and if they had, they had not seen one quite like that. They would gather around in small groups, looking at it, wondering what to do with it. There were a few who were cheered by its beauty. Of those, some were changed by it. Most people, however, were merely bewildered. They did not know what to make of the flower.

So they just left it alone and thought they would get used to it. But they did not. It was so conspicuous.. It showed up the drabness, the desolation, all around for what it was: empty, ugly, dead. It became intolerable. You must not blame them. You or I would have done the same, feeling as they did. One evening they went out in a great crowd to the bomb site and they trampled on that sunflower and beat it to the ground, and crushed its petals till they were but a stain which the dust soon covered. They went away in silence, their job done.

Yet they destroyed that strange plant in high summer, when its flower was full of ripe seed. In their dance of death they scattered that seed over the entire bomb site and buried some of it in the ground. So it was that next spring the bomb site at the end of Jubilee Street was covered with sunflowers.

Trevor Dennis

Pray with our partners worldwide using the photographs in the CWM insert.

Read: Isaiah 58:5-12

Lord Jesus Christ,
you ask us to follow in your way,
to take up your cross
and carry it to Jerusalem.

We confess that giving up chocolate, smoking or alcohol
is not taking up your cross.
We confess our self-righteous attempts at following you.

Instead give us the willpower to truly take up your cross.
Grant us courage to break the chains of injustice,
to set free the oppressed,
to share food with the hungry,
to open our homes to the homeless,
to clothe the naked,
to care for family and stranger alike.

Lord Jesus Christ,
carrying your cross means having a new perspective on life,
new priorities and life-choices,
loving our neighbour as we love ourselves,
journeying with you not just for Lent but every day of our lives.

Ash Wednesday

'Oh where are you going
and can I come with you?'

In our journey through Lent to Easter this year we will reflect on places; the ones Jesus visited and places we go to. The gospel narrative often includes 'stage directions' like; 'He went up a mountain', 'He crossed to the other side of the lake', 'He entered a village'. Reflecting on places will give us an opportunity to be physical as well as spiritual. When you go to another place, a different place, a new place, there are new things to notice and to do, new people to relate to. A wandering ministry like the one Jesus had is so different from the static life-style that many people lead, who are probably used to one place, one community, one situation. However, to relate to different places, communities and situations is a feature of the lives of many people. In reflecting on where Jesus went we will also think about places he invites us to go to on our journey. One of the ways of doing this is by making a Lent book. For each week of Lent you will need a piece of A4 paper folded in half. Using the phrases in italics given for each week, we will build up our reflection on places so that by the end of Lent we have our own record of our journey through Lent this year.

In your group, make a list of those who may be more familiar with a travelling, wandering, moving life-style.
For example:

long distance lorry drivers, refugees and asylum seekers, 'traveller' families, merchant seafarers, circus and fairground workers.

Get a large map, which could be of your region or country, and using some appropriate symbols to represent the folk you have named, place them on the map in appropriate places:
a toy caravan could represent traveller families living at the local authority site, a toy lorry at the motorway service station for the lorry drivers. If you have no objects to use then a small picture or a photograph cut out of a magazine could be used.
Spend some time together in prayer for people on the move.

Pray with *partner churches in Northern Ireland and those working for regeneration.*

37

Lord Jesus Christ,
in the loneliness of the wilderness you were tested by
offers of food, offers of power, and challenged to reveal who you were.
You did not give into temptation despite the loneliness.

In the wilderness of our lives, when we feel lonely and isolated,
help us to resist the temptations we encounter,
> when we want to find solace in material things,
> when we want to find ourselves in dominating others
> when we want to say, 'I do not know this man from Nazareth.'

In the familiarity of being the church, where we feel safe and
comfortable
help us to resist the temptations we encounter,
> when we want to take refuge in our traditional way of doing
> things,
> when we allow money to limit the nature of our witness,
> when we accept others only if they conform to our expectations
> and conditions.

Help us to turn once again to you.
Strengthen us when our commitment is weak.
Give us vision to see how we may participate in your Kingdom.
Enable us to put our trust in you.

a good place I was alone...

I have eaten in America.
I have been to Australia.
I have changed my ways in Fuji.
I have been mobbed in Guam.
I have cooked in the Cook Islands.
I have sneezed in the Marshal Islands.
I have damaged what was on Nauru.
I have fainted in New Caledonia.
I have woken up to a New Zealand dawn.
I have fried fish in Japan.
I have eaten fish in the Solomon Islands.
I have tempted fish in Tuvalu.
I have been lost in Vanuatu....
I have wandered far and wide.
I know very well that my land has nothing.
Its beauty lies within me.
Not on its surface or wherever.
There is none better than my land.
None.

Teweiariki Francis Teaero, from Kiribati

a bad place I was alone....

'I thought, we're never going to get over this, we've ruined our life.
My Health Visitor offered to sit with me and talk through things. '
'New mums are supposed to be happy, aren't they? '
'When we separated, his mother stopped seeing them. She didn't
even send birthday cards.'
'It was like a kick in the guts'.
'If I don't get an evening out this week, I'm going to start climbing
the walls'.

Parents involved in Surestart speaking about their experiences.

Pray with partner churches in Kiribati and Tuvalu.

Read: Psalm 27 especially verses 1 & 14.

In the darkness I cry to you.

Keep watch for God who is our light and hope.

In the busyness of life, when there is no time or order,

Keep watch for God who is our light and hope.

In the emptiness of life, when meaning escapes me,

Keep watch for God who is our light and hope.

In the loneliness of life, when I am singing a different song from all around me,

Keep watch for God who is our light and hope.

In the sadness of life, when pain and grief overwhelm me,

Keep watch for God who is our light and hope.

In the uncertainty of life, when all is strange and disorientating,

Keep watch for God who is our light and hope.

In the excitement of life, when new adventures and opportunities abound,

Keep watch for God who is our light and hope.

In the happiness of life, when my living overflows with joy,

Keep watch for God who is our light and hope.

In the entirety of my living.

Keep watch for God who is our light and hope.

I turned back....

As refugees,
we are victims of violence and war.
We left our motherland
because we were being mistreated in many ways.
We ran to get protection in other countries....
Give us peace,
to return back to our beloved country,
our previous heaven, Sudan.
Give us our ancestors' land.
Africa, live in peace forever!

Andrew Mayak, a refugee from Sudan living in Kenya

I leapt forward....

Nine-year-old Bintu Amara has had to become self-reliant. She had
to have her foot amputated after she was shot by rebels in the
January 1999 invasion of Freetown, Sierre Leone. The war has
devastated Sierre Leone - the country with the lowest levels of
income, education and life expectancy in the world - and left many
people emotionally scarred. In the same attack which injured Bintu,
her father was shot in the foot, and her mother and sister both had
one hand chopped off. Her three-year-old sister had her whole
right arm chopped off. Bintu is staying in an amputee camp and
has to walk a mile to and from school everyday, but she is
determined to do this. She is one of the brightest in her class and
when she grows up she wants to be a teacher saying: "If I become
a teacher I won't forget what I have learned, and I can carry on
learning more".

Christian Aid

Pray with **partner churches in west, east and north Africa.**

Read: Psalm 68:1-8; 1 Corinthians 10:13b

Protecting God,
draw your wings close around me,
in the midst of my fear,
in the times of trial and testing.

As a mother hen settles herself upon her chicks
nestle in around me
so I am snuggled by your compassion.

As a mother elephant keeps her calf
beneath her body as they walk along together,
guide me in your ways,
do not let me stray from you
until I too have the strength and maturity to walk independently.

As a mother lion feeds her cubs
so they may grow strong and healthy,
feed me with your Word so I may discern your will
and find my way
through darkness to light
through trial and testing to peace.

Protecting God,
draw your wings close around me.

Slides could be used to visually
accompany this prayer. The slides
could depict the images in the prayer
i.e. a bird with outstretched wings; a hen
with chicks, an elephant, a lion and a bird
with outstretched wings, or you may like to
choose other images which portray the ideas
of protection, compassion, guidance, and feeding.

Lent 3

a difficult place.....

"There can be no doubt that the grinding poverty of well over half of all families in Zimbabwe contributes towards building up social tensions; and that the lack of training is one major factor for the rising poverty".

Director of Silvera House

Silvera House is a training centre which was established by the Jesuits in 1964, to offer assistance for the poor. It offers a range of training opportunities for young men and women in industrial relations, primary health care, civic education, commerce, appropriate technology, building, carpentry, crafts, dressmaking and sustainable agriculture. The sustainable agriculture course is based on teaching traditional farming skills and careful water husbandry, with the long-term aim of decreasing the use of chemicals and pesticides (which are imported and expensive) and to encourage reversion to organic farming methods.

Commitment for Life

an enjoyable place.....

Skills for People

This is the top place in the North East. I come to *Skills* to meet up and talk to people. It's friendly. I love travelling here. I did right to come here. There are nice people here.

David Locke

Key house (project headquarters) is great. It has lifts for wheelchairs. We can pop in when we like and we answer the phones.

Julie Anderson

I love it at *Skills*. I learned nothing at school, but I taught myself to read. I've learned lots at *Skills*. I tell my story, and I write poetry.

Ann Clark

At *Skills* we learn to speak up for ourselves. I collect money for refreshments at the Drop-In. It's a big step for me.

Irene Edwards.

These comments are by people who are involved in *Skills for People*, a project begun by, and still supported by, Jesmond URC.

We have to wait at the pelican crossing for a matter of half a minute and all around we can see the different cultures in the area, in the children and their parents. I feel the heart of God must rejoice at the sight of all God's people together.

Inderjit Bhogal

Pray with partner churches in Wales and for those working for regeneration.

Read: Luke 15:1-3; 11b-32

Voice 1   'Kill the fatted calf'. Find the best robe
Adorn him with jewels. Put shoes on his feet'

Voice 2   The son who was lost has come home.
The child who had chosen his own way has returned.
The family, which was broken, is complete again.

Voice 1   'Father I have sinned against God and against you.
I am no longer fit to be called your child.'

Voice 2   The son who was lost is now found.
The child who was dead has returned to life
Let the feasting begin; the son has come home.

Voice 3   Parent God, you are always there,
waiting to welcome us home with open arms,
offering us your unconditional love,
drawing us back into your family once again.

Forgive us when our arrogance, fear or shame
keep us apart from you.
Help us to accept that we are worthy to receive
all you have promised us.
Guide us along the path which leads to home.

a good place to be....

My small farm is managed as a serious enterprise, but I am unashamedly romantic about the countryside. The concept of 'sustainability' not only embraces the environment, but also the landscape and a set of dwindling social structures and traditions, all under threat. When birds sing and butterflies drift across flowering hedgerows, I not only rejoice that the local ecology has not yet been destroyed: my heart sings with exultation.

Jonathan Dimbleby

a place to start again....

Since 1986 Shigeru Ban has built at least nine different types of cardboard structures, from simple garden shelters to permanent outdoor dwellings and even a paper church. A turning point came in 1995 with the Kobe earthquake in his native Japan. Walking through the city's devastated suburbs, Ban was shocked by the survivors' privations. He quickly made plans to build a community hall from paper logs. Once built it soon metamorphosed into a place of worship. He then built a further 30 paper log dwellings to house the remainder of the residents. Each cost a mere Y250,000 (that's £1,500 each).

Jon Pratty

Pray with partner churches in Madagascar engaged in efforts to restore and treasure the earth.

Read: John 12:1-8

Generous God,
forgive us, when like Judas, we calculate our response to you,
when we seek our own gain above the good of others,
when we don't understand the extravagance of other people's faith.

Generous God, forgive us.

Loving God,
help us to learn from Mary's actions.
Enable us to give as generously as she gave
with no thought of reward or recognition,
with no embarrassment or hesitation.

Loving God, enable us to give.

Welcoming God,
Open us to accept others as Jesus accepted Mary.
Challenge us to accept the generosity of others
especially when we feel we are better than the giver.
Make us quick to speak for those whom others want to dismiss,
Help us to show our appreciation to all who show us kindness.

Welcoming God, help us accept others as you have accepted us.

a place I feel welcome....

"A Kurdish refugee family was moved up from London yesterday and there's only one other Kurdish speaking family in this city. I tried to take a cot round for the baby. It was rather large and I got it stuck in the car and couldn't get it out again when I got there".

Local community health worker, Sheffield

Reflect on what your church, together with other local churches, could actually do to make asylum seekers feel welcome in your area and to give practical help. Pray for the asylum seekers and refugees, pray about the situation in their homelands and their difficulties in this country. Pray that your local community can be open and welcoming, whatever the local conditions may be.

However efficient the new system is in delivering food and accommodation (to asylum seekers and refugees), it cannot deliver friendship. Consider setting up a befriending scheme so that local asylum seekers will know that there are sympathetic local residents to whom they can turn.

Churches' Commission for Racial Justice

a place I welcome others....

Hope Flowers school was founded by Hussein Issa, a Muslim, as a place where poor Palestinian children could share education and other opportunities with Israeli children. He said 'Peace and democracy education should be given to infants with their mother's milk'. For Issa, education covered all aspects of life and the Hope Flowers school grew from one rented room with 22 children and no chairs within five years to a primary and secondary school west of Bethlehem, in al-Khader. Christian and Muslim pupils learned side by side and mixed with Jewish pupils from other schools. They learned about reconciliation, democracy and peace, as did their parents when the school hosted meetings in 1996 to introduce local people to the process of the first Palestinian Council elections. Chickens were raised and plants grown and in every respect the school sought to live up to its name: 'Hope Flowers'.

Pray with refugees and asylum seekers worldwide.

Read: **Psalm 118:1; Luke 19:35-40**

Yes, God!
This is the day, the time and the place:
We can feel it, we know it.
Today is more than a festival,
more than a "flavour of the month" following.
Today you come into our lives
into our everyday way of doing things
and promise to confront the unfairness of our world.
So from today we'll tell the world:

God's love, it lasts for ever.

It's great God!
The way you've sent your Son today:
we can see the special signs.
This way of coming into things,
not an aggressive take-over, "sorted" style.
Today you come into our lives,
into who we are in what we do,
and share a living parable of humble leadership.
So from today we'll live to say:

God's love, it lasts for ever.

Here's God in Christ!
Our God sent, saving grace:
come living Saviour, you're just who we need.
Cut through the politicians words.
Speak out in hard commercial places.
Show the world the truth we too must learn:

God's love, it lasts for ever.

Palm Sunday

Take just a moment in time
to reflect at this Spring resurrection time.
Pause to hear the silent sounds,
the panting and groaning of Wisdom as she births creation,
new shoots, buds and seedlings,
the jubilant peeling of silent bells ever so faintly echoed in the
spring chorus.
Take just a moment in time
to recognise that this is a kairos moment;
it is opportunity that is birthed today.
Take just a moment in time
to reflect that we, the dancers, the Fool's people,
have been created to nurture the dreams and aspirations
of all those who planted these opportunities.
Join the Jester's dance, the commonweal not of clowns but of fools,
simply listen out for the silent sounds, the noiseless ringing
heard only by fools - the dreamers of dreams and visionaries.

Helen M Mee

Take just a moment in time....
* to look at your Lent book,
* to reflect on the places or places you have visited,
* to reflect on the places you inhabit now,
* to remember the companions, particularly those prophets
  and visionaries, you have had and have now in those
  places.

Take a pot or jar and place in it a branch, a twig, a leaf or
flower to represent some of those places and people. Place it
with your Lent book in a sunny place until Easter Sunday.

Pray with **partner churches in Samoa and American Samoa.**

Introduction to Holy Week

We continue the theme of places into Holy Week. Try to visit some of the places suggested this week. If you can't visit all or any of them, then try to think about the places you do go to. Perhaps they are places you always visit at this time of year or even everyday. Try to see them as if you were visiting for the first time or ask yourself how would a stranger see this place, or a child? If you are going to the church you usually attend during the week try to see it as if visiting for the first time too. Think about this parable.....

The parable of the badly maintained house

There once was a badly maintained house in a delightful suburb. The people who lived in it were very nice: kind to others, friendly if anyone called, helpful in the neighbourhood, and generous to people in need, even those not in their street. The house itself was in a sorry state. The windows at the front were boarded up which made the house look dark and uninviting. The front door wasn't at the front, but at the side, and no one coming to that house for the first time would know how to get in because it just wasn't obvious. There was a high narrow gate and an even higher wall which made it almost impossible to see into the garden. The garden itself was overgrown with weeds and the path was a death trap. Besides which the path didn't even lead to the front door but took some round about overgrown route round to the dimly lit back entrance.

Of course the people who lived in the house knew all of this. They knew how to avoid the gaps in the path and the brambles. They always took a torch with them and made sure never to be trying to get in late at night. They often wondered why they didn't have many visitors. They always said they would welcome any who come, but very few managed to negotiate the gate, the path and the garden, let alone find the door.

The family got older and older and fewer and fewer. Still they could not understand why more visitors didn't call. What will happen to the house and to the few people who still live in it? If you have brains then use them!

Janet Lees

Read: Isaiah 42:1-3; Psalm 36:5-7; John 12:1-8

Here I am, this holy Monday morning,
torn between the love you call out of me
and the demands life puts upon me.

In my heart I want
to give myself to serving you:
to making all I am and everything I own
an act of loving commitment;
to respond to your acceptance of me
with a significant act of devotion.

In my head I've got
to give myself to what I do:
to being a team player, meeting deadlines,
reaching targets, performing well.
I've got to be strong, play politics,
position myself for higher grading
through significant acts of devotion.

Must this Monday really wreck me?
Must this heart and head be poles apart?
Show me God of all my life
how to serve you in what I do.
Let me seek the living Christ this very day,
and see me now as where you are.

And on this holy Monday,
make my devotion and doing
one single act of Christian living:
a pouring out of my most treasured gifts
in love for you.

Monday of Holy Week

Do: **Have a meal, alone or with others.**
The sacred meal is at the heart of most religions. Yet, it is often eating
together, the communal meal, that suffers in our lives: pressure,
harmonising different work schedules, the TV programmes and so on.
I think we have to capture the sacramental imagination through some,
poem, mythic narrative - to recover the sacred power of eating together.

Mary Grey

Bread. A clean sky. Active peace. A woman's voice singing somewhere,
melody drifting like smoke from the cook fires. The army disbanded, the
harvest abundant. The wound healed, the child wanted, the prisoner
freed, the body's integrity honoured, the lover returned...The labour
equal, fair and valued. Delight in the challenge for consensus to solve
problems. No hand raised in any gesture but greeting. Secure interiors -
of heart, home, land - so firm as to make secure borders irrelevant at last.
And everywhere laughter, care, dancing, contentment. A humble, earthly
paradise in the now.

A Women's Creed from Beijing

He's the one
He didn't write me off, or throw stones
He didn't kick me when I was down
who touched the heart of who I am,
and called from me my longing
to find myself and give my all.

Everything I've saved and stored,
has different value now I'm close to him.
This Christ makes ownership a different thing,
redeems me with a gentle strength
that has me washing feet.

He's the one I'd have done anything for:
who saw the very heart of what I did,
and called for me to follow:
lift God's poor
reinstate God's law
shatter domination.
Everything I want loses its significance
in silly talk of sacrificial service.
I'll use what I value most,
and refuse to hear what I value least,
to get what I want.

She's the one who understands:
who shares God's vision in my life

*Pray with
partner churches in the
North-west region of
England and those
working for regeneration.*

Chris Warner

Too slight a task

Limitless God,
forgive us when we limit ourselves
to saving the church instead of serving you.

We have misinterpreted your word,
believing your promised refuge
to be a place to hide,
your recognition of us in old age
to be permission to retire,
your presence when our strength fails
as an acceptance that we can go no further.

Yet you challenge us to think again:
to find safety in active discipleship,
to search our years for wisdom and experience,
to see our weakness as your greatest strength.
It is too slight a task, you say,
that we should be content with church life
while a whole world struggles on
not seeing how your good news
illuminates a shared journey.

This holy week requires our moving forward:
our growing out of growing in,
and growing up in you.
You dare us die to all our insecurities.
You promise life beyond the death we fear.

Wise God, all our instincts tell us
that the journey of this week is foolish.
Help us to believe that if we trust you
you can use us to change the world.

Do: **Visit a place of refuge. This might be a day centre, a night shelter, a retreat centre, a holiday home, a cave, a community centre.**

The summer programme at Llandecwyn (between Harlech and Porthmodog near the Welsh coast) for the year 2000 was a pilot project to discover whether small churches and chapels which are unlikely to be the centre of community life again, some of them in isolated places, some in the middle of towns and cities, can become places of pilgrim prayer - quiet, welcoming, offering resources for spiritual exploration and nourishment.

Llandecwyn has its roots deep in Welsh Christianity and its more recent shape in the Anglican tradition. But in its simplicity it could be a place where people of different denominations, and indeed of different faiths and none, might find an atmosphere in which to breathe freely - in reflection, in meditation, in prayer, in quiet conversation - without feeling that they were going to be pressured into a system of believing that no longer seems to connect with their lives.

The church has been open for a few weeks each of the last few summers. Interest in the project is growing, as are requests from other places where people are asking similar questions. It is time now to take a jump, if not a leap, of faith.

Jim Cotter

Pray with *partner churches in Myanmar (Burma).*

Read: Isaiah 50:4-9a; Hebrews 12:1-2; John13:21-26

Betrayed Saviour,
when someone betrays us
let us see you in that room
amongst your friends
and knowing who would turn you in.

Let us see your sadness
and your strength,
your sharing bread with one
who soon would share a kiss
and walk away.

Do: **Visit the local job centre.**

A visit to a job centre in Sheffield in March 2000 revealed the following:
* there were 883 vacancies on display, of which 12 were standing adverts for enlistment in the forces, and 52 were for training places, most of which were on a benefit plus £10 weekly allowance basis,
* median hourly pay, where this could be calculated, was £4.00, mean hourly pay was £4.40, part time hourly pay, at a mean of £4.13, was lower than full time, at a mean of £4.91,
* hourly pay available to new entrants to jobs advertised in Sheffield's Job Centre is low; the median of £4.00 per hour is well below the national average and only 11% above the minimum wage,
* 35% were part time (less than 30 hours per week), and 49% were full time (30 hours or more), 16% were unknown,
* between a fifth and a third of all vacancies were advertised at the Minimum Wage for adults; the Minimum Wage has therefore had a significant impact on the kinds of jobs advertised through Job Centres,
* nearly a quarter of jobs yielded weekly pay less than the Employer's National Insurance threshold of £67: this is the level at which a number of rights kick in, irrespective of earnings from other jobs, people with these jobs would be at a significant disadvantage,
* all the evidence is that the total of vacancies in Sheffield still numbers considerably less than the 15,000 claimant count.

Bob Warwicker

Use the descriptions of jobs and people on the facing page to pray with people from your local community.

Read: 1 Corinthians 11:23-26; John 13:1-17, 34

At a playscheme in Germany we spent a whole week building houses together. We made a whole town in the park, with wood and cardboard, strong staples and buckets of brightly coloured paint. At the end of each day we were hot and tired and covered in emulsion. Then the buckets and hose pipes came out. And for half an hour we threw water at each other. The children had the hose pipes, the playworkers had the buckets. I remember one of the female leaders standing to one side. This sort of thing wasn't for her, not until I threw the first bucket of water over her. Once that well groomed hair was drenched she screamed and chased and laughed with all the rest of us. No leader escaped the hoses, each child was clean of paint and dirt. And soon the sun had dried us all, and we longed for the next day and more building to do.

Help us humble Christ
to wash each other as we work
to build a faith community.

Let no one stand aside,
too proud or shy to share the joy
of mutual Christ-like caring.

May all of us, whatever age,
be open to your cleansing love
then you will be our food and drink.

We pray that as we share this meal
We'll learn the new command you give
that by the way we grow in love
we'll show that we belong to you.

Exodus 12:1-4, (5-10), 11-14
Psalm 116:1-2,12-19
1 Corinthians 11:23-26 John 13:1-17, 31b-35

Holy Thursday

Do: **Visit a playgroup, playscheme, under-fives group, after school club, playground or other play facility.**

I like it when we do communion

Kathy, 8

I adore family services because you get to stay with your family. You get to receive bread and juice. It's great fun.

Lilian Brown

I like the family service because I like to receive the bread. I also like to stay with my parents and listen to readings. I dislike the long sermon; it's so boring. Apart from that I really enjoy it.

Natalie

I like family service because you get bread and wine.

Matthew

I like it when we make things like the Easter garden.

I like it when we get to help with the collection; get to have Communion; sing lively hymns; go and help the minister. I don't like it when we get asked questions we don't understand; or don't get pictures or something to talk about at the front.

Emily Booth, 8

I wish we could say prayers we have made.
Claire, 4   What do Children Think? URCHIN

I can't wait until Sunday. The service is going to be really exciting!
Hannah, 6

Oh good, we're having bread and juice again today. We do it 'cos we like Jesus.

Lauren, 4

I do hope it's Communion, I really do.

Luke, 5   Shiregreen URC

Pray with partner churches working with children and young people in holiday playschemes.

59

Read: John 18:1-19:42

Who is it you want?
When I see someone coming
wanting to take my time or money,
will I go to meet them?
Will I let someone else protect me?

Are you one of his followers?
When I hear someone ask me
whose side I'm on and what I think,
will I deny what I hold dear?
or speak of what the gospel says?

What charge do you bring?
When I am in the crowd
and someone speaks out seeking right,
will I back up the lonely voice?
Will I take risks and stand with Christ?

Away with him!
When all my group unite
to stand against a righteous cause,
will I resign and walk away?
Will I stay on and speak my mind?

It is accomplished!
Crucified Christ
Whatever choice I make today,
however weak or strong I feel,
work for me still until the day
that I am fully one with you.

Good Friday

Do: **Visit the local rubbish tip. How does it smell and sound? Who is also there?**

In an 'upside-down kingdom', God is not there to answer our questions, but rather to question our answers.
God gave the world Number One Status 2000 years ago when he gave up his Son, who was sacrificed on a run-down area's rubbish-tip outside a city. A rubbish-tip with its scavengers in modern India, like Golgotha, is given its own dignity by the Son of Man.

Murdoch MacKenzie

"True, the elephant is stronger. But the ants.... well, there are more of them".
We are women. We are mothers. Our children have been taken away and we do not know where they are. Where were they taken? Where did they put them? Are they alive? Are they dead? And we started to ask, here and there. In hospitals and police stations, to the church and to the authorities. Nobody answers.

"Mad women of Palza de Mayo", we were called. Mad women, indeed, but with the madness of ants attacking the elephant of brute force.
When Jesus was crucified, there was a crowd around; and his acquaintances, including the women who had followed him from Galilee, stood at a distance watching. They did not run away.
The text does not put words in their mouth, but they were there; they were afraid, but they witnessed the horror, they accompanied their beloved one and defied the powerful with their presence.
They expressed their resistance by being together and not giving up, in the middle of death. Let us remember all those women and men all over the world who, even without spoken words today, still shout out for justice and stand by the oppressed, aware that there are other Christs, the victims of new crucifixions.

Ana Villanueva

Pray with partner churches working with people who are alone or who feel abandoned.

We'd like to lay to rest, crucified Christ,
the thought that we'd participate:
in thoughts and actions
that would lead to this
bleak Saturday

But if we're honest we can't.

We'd like to lay to rest, life-lost Christ,
the thought that we have made you life-less:
entombed you and sealed you
in the safe services and romantic story-telling,
of Church life

But, to tell the truth, we can't.

We'd like to lay to rest, buried Christ,
the thought that we are simply here on guard:
in case someone should come and steal
what we have cared for, perfumed, wrapped
in our traditions

But, of course, we can't

We'd like to lay to rest this night
our fears and tears and hiding:
throw off our self protective ways
and be community

So that tomorrow we can rise with you.

Job 14:1-14   1 Peter 4:1-8
Psalm: 31:1-4, 15-16
Matthew 27:57-66

Holy Saturday

Do: **Visit an old cemetery. Walk around and look at the graves, the stones and statues, the names and engravings.**

On the day I wrote this prayer I was in Mainz, Germany, at a centre next to an enormous cemetery. I went to explore and found rows of large structures, mausoleum-like with iron gates and steps leading down to crypts below. Everything was heavy: each family plot, its boundaries set in stone, with its own unique way of holding up the names of those now buried there. Some were beautifully carved with intricate patterns and promises, heavenly hosts or heart breaking scenes of a broken Christ is his mother's arms. There were rugged stones; simple rock shapes covered with ivy. There were many little gates protecting narrow entrances to stone shelved resting places.

It suddenly occurred to me that Jesus was laid in such a structure: rock-carved, a narrow entrance and a stone door, a wealthy tomb. Once more a paradox: his short life from stable to sarcophagus. Once more a well-meant misunderstanding of where to place this Jesus, this carpenter turned teacher.

An each gate there was a chain and padlock, rusty or renewed, all heavy and strong. Were these for keeping in or keeping out? Despite myself, I see that here's a place where fantasy and superstition can grow. Each gate attracts the eye of the fearful or curious. Would you dare to enter if the locks were gone and the gates open? But, just in case, the lock remain, though the guards have now gone (to save money). The biggest danger now is the loss of antique stones, stolen by collectors for their own homes. This Saturday's a waiting day, a wondering day, a weary day. What do you see in an old cemetery, as you wait, wondering where a heavy heart will find new life?

Chris Warner

Pray with those who work to maintain church gardens and graveyards as places of calm and quiet.

Read: Isaiah 65:17-25; Acts 10:34-43; Luke 24:1-12

What nonsense God, what wonderful nonsense,
we can't believe it - daren't believe it
it's a prophet's babbling!
no more babies dying and young men in burial bags;
no more growing cash crops and going hungry;
no more working day in, day out, for nothing;
no more living without any hope of a future;
what wonderful nonsense!
I'll sing that song of hope.

What nonsense God, what wonderful nonsense,
we can't believe it - daren't believe it
it's a woman's story telling!
no more mourning our dead with endless grieving;
no more thinking oppressors will always hold power;
no more thinking our lot is the way you ordained it;
no more living today without hope for the rest;
what wonderful nonsense!
I'll live this life in faith.

What nonsense God, what wonderful nonsense,
we can't believe it - daren't believe it
it's a disciple's desperation!
no more favourites in God's eyes;
no more living in fear of the people who hurt us;
no more seeing injustice and watching in silence;
no more making mistakes without hope of forgiveness;
what wonderful nonsense!
I'll trust it from today.

Isaiah 65:17-25
Psalm 118:1-2, 14-24
Acts 10:34-43   Luke 24:1-12

Easter Day

In August 1869, the Archbishop of York consecrated a new parish church in the expanding middle-class suburb of Sharrow, in Sheffield. St Andrew's fine broach spire dominated the neighbourhood, and anyone who was anyone was to be seen in its pews; there was room for 700 people in its dignified nave, chancel and transepts. In January 2000, with the nave, chancel and transepts already demolished, the spire has been finally removed forever from the Sheffield sky-line.

I ask myself, when did death become inevitable? Was it the moment in 1996 when the church council and I faced our lack of will to continue the unequal struggle to save a building plagued with structural faults. A week before Christmas our insurers would no longer cover us for worship in an unsound building. We moved into the church hall.

In the early 1990s older parishioners still thought of the church interior as "beautiful". Yet the reality was of scruffy, ageing, ill-fitting pews, of hideous 50s strip lighting, of meaningless empty spaces where excess pews had been removed and of general clutter and mess. All that without glancing up to the threatening cracks above.

Or was the death of the church actually written into its conception in 1867? Robin Gill has shown in 'The Myth of the Empty Church' how competitive building between Anglicans and Methodists in the latter part of the 19th century created more church seating than there were people, thus guaranteeing half-empty churches and contributing to their eventual decline.

Certainly it might seem that the death of a church building would mark the nadir of that long descent. But strangely, it is not so. For facing reality and refusing to cling to the past give new energy and new life. Our congregation has joined up with our nearest Methodist church in their building, and there is now life and hope and creativity among a membership of some 200 Christians who have once again got a do-able project and the possibility of a more modest, searching, serving Christianity.

I walk past the demolition site once again. I think I understand why it was inevitable. And I have found out that there is life after death.

Nicholas Jowett
St Andrews, Psalter Lane is a joint Methodist-Anglican church in Sheffield.

Pray with partner churches where the challenges and tasks seem impossible.

Read: John 20:19-29; Revelation 1:4-8

God, your vision of us is amazing.
When we look at the church
we see a frightened handful of people
hiding from the world,
afraid of shadows.
You see a royal dynasty
free and powerful.

We see people who have almost given up believing
anything that can't be seen,
who want hard evidence
before making a commitment.
You see faithful priests
holding the people before God.

From where we stand, the church seems half-dead -
fewer people than ever before
older congregations
crumbling buildings
words that no-one understands
ideas no-one believes in any more.

Into our fear you breathe peace;
To our doubt you open your broken hands
and faith and life surge through us.

God, you are here and now
You have always been
You will always be
Sovereign Lord of all.
Alpha and Omega,
through our unimpressive beginnings
You achieve your ends.

Acts 5:27-32   Psalm 118:14-29
Revelation 1:4-8
John 20:19-31

Easter 2

....'look at my hands'.

At a conference organised by a large missionary society, the Director reported on how much effort his society had put in to opening a modern hospital in the Philippines. He spoke of the splendid opening service and the praise which had been heaped on the society by the government representative. Whilst the dignitaries were touring the much acclaimed accident and emergency department, the first patient was carried in. It was a young boy around 13 years of age. He had got his hand caught in factory machinery. His frantic efforts to free his trapped hand had led to him trapping his other hand. He came to the hospital having lost both hands. The Director was courageous enough to ask the question whether the missionary society had chosen appropriately in investing all its resources in the hospital. Perhaps the wiser priority might have been to provide guards for factory machinery and campaigns for improved safety laws.

Ann Morisy

In a group, or alone, look at hands; those of group members or from photographs. Reflect on what they do. End by joining them together, holding hands however this is possible, for several minutes.

Pray for the 'Belonging to the World Church' programme, that it might help us see ourselves as others see us.

Read: **John 21:1-19; Revelation 5:11-14**

Early morning meeting at a lakeside
conference centre
or at a business breakfast;
unexpected meetings on the road
or on the train;
formal meetings at boardroom tables,
video conferences and satellite links.

Simple sharing
of work and food and stories
and the heart's need shared silently.

Massed choirs and grave procession
and myriad, myriad creatures
who meet with no other purpose
than to contemplate the greatness,
the power and the glory
of God.

God of all meetings and encounters,
we pray for all who will sit in meetings today.
If they meet to do business, give clarity
and honesty in their commerce,
wisdom in hard decisions.
If they meet to give and receive counsel,
give tenderness in judgement,
support in despair.
And where people meet to worship
give such a sense of your presence
that in all our meetings we recognise you
and your love and justice and goodness
are known and shared.

Acts 9:1-6,(7-20)   Psalm 30
Revelation 5:11-14
John 21:1-19

Easter 3

Disciple 1: Is this the meeting of the Disciples of Jesus Executive Committee?
Disciple 2: Yes, it is and you're late! Don't you remember he said 'I am going to meet with you in Galilee'?
Disciple 1: Well yes, but I took the scenic route.
Disciple 3: Are we all here now?
Disciple 4: Looks like it. All here except the Chair that is.
Disciple 3: He'll be here. He said 'when two or three of you have a meeting, I'll be there', and there's more than two or three of us here'.
Disciple 5: Yes, but he's not been at every meeting recently, has he?
Disciple 6: He was at the subcommittee meeting we had in Emmaus a couple of weeks ago.
Disciple 7: I don't remember him ever missing a meeting I've been at. I've missed a few myself of course.
Disciple 5: Well we all do from time to time. I mean, maybe we can't expect him to keep turning up to them all now.
Disciple 6: What do you mean now?
Disciple 5: After that meeting at Golgotha, when he said 'It is finished'. Perhaps he's not coming to any more.
Disciple 3: He's coming all right. He's the one who really makes things happen at meetings.

At the beginning of a meeting this week.....
Read the conversation between the disciples, making sure that those who have speaking parts represent the range of people at the meeting; women and men, young and old, black and white or whatever range of people are at the meeting. Reflect on what the disciples say. In what way have you know the Risen Christ present at your meetings since Easter? What are the signs he is present at a meeting and what are the signs he is absent? In what way does Jesus continue to 'make things happen' at your meetings?

Janet Lees

Pray for energy in meetings.

Read: Acts 9:36-43; John 10:22-30;
        Revelation 7:9-17

It is hard to believe, God,
the notion of resurrection.
Death is very real.

Here is the bundle of exquisitely sewn clothes
made with such love, still with her smell and feel,
but now her hands lie quiet
on her dead breast.

Here is his place, his empty chair, his tools,
the half-made artefacts he will not now complete.
He lies in earth, strong arms untimely still,
his sisters desolate.

Here's where she spoke of justice, stood for truth
until one night they came for her with guns.
Her voice is still, her body broken
in some unmarked grave.

These are they who have passed through the great ordeal;
... God will wipe every tear from their eyes.

God of all comfort,
wipe the tears from our eyes too.
Help us to see that the hard reality of death
is conquered by the love that lives for ever,
the faith that looks for glimpses of life and hope,
and the truth of God's good news of justice and love.
Through Jesus Christ, risen and alive today.

2001

Praying with CWM Churches

Nick Sireau

Please use this leaflet as a part of your prayer life. Suggestions for prayer can be supplemented and updated by using the prayer section of CWM's journal, Inside Out, available from your church offices.

EUROPE

United Reformed Church (URC)
(with the Congregational Union of Scotland as the Synod of Scotland)

Give thanks for:
✦ The ministry of Tony Burnham who retires as general secretary in July 2001;

✦ The growing partnership between UK congregations and overseas partner churches;

✦ The union with the Congregational Union of Scotland (CUS) in April 2000;

✦ New developments in training to be a church in mission.

Pray for:
✦ David Cornick who takes over as general secretary in July 2001;

✦ New efforts to address issues of racial justice within the Church and society;

✦ The many new local mission initiatives launched each year;

✦ The Belonging to the World Church programme.

URC and CUS leaders light a symbolic candle at the ceremony uniting both churches.

Presbyterian Church of Wales (PCW)

Give thanks for:
✦ The mission partners within the PCW, some holding ecumenical appointments and many working in difficult situations in chaplaincies, community work, mission enabling, youth and children's work;

✦ The restructuring within the PCW's South Wales area and for signs of movement and development there.

Pray for:
✦ The continued development of work in South Wales;

✦ The successful appointment of more mission partners, many working with small and ageing congregations;

✦ The PCW to be faithful in its witness to the kingdom of God.

Congregational Federation (CF)

Pray for:

✦ The network of mission enablers seeking to work with groups of churches to develop their mission. The network includes two members from CWM partner churches;

✦ The Integrated Training Course as it seeks to equip people for ministry within the church;

✦ The denomination's new structures and the new general secretary, Rev Michael Heaney, who started in July 2000;

✦ Local churches to be welcoming and relevant to their local communities.

Union of Welsh Independents (UWI)

Please pray that:

✦ A comprehensive missionary programme be devised for young people to equip them to present Christ to their contemporaries and to train them to be leaders;

✦ The churches will become, once more, living communities with a real interest in people and their worth before God, and that they will reach out to those who have lost their faith;

✦ The leadership of mission enabler Rev Hmar Sangkhuma bear fruit as the UWI begins to listen to him;

✦ The churches will be a source of blessing in their communities.

Reformed Churches in the Netherlands (RCN)

Please pray that:

✦ The unity between the three uniting churches, among them the Reformed Churches in the Netherlands, may grow at the national and local levels, despite the many difficulties ahead;

✦ The secular people of the Netherlands may meet God, the Father of Jesus Christ;

✦ People who are released from prison can make a new beginning in the Exodus Houses founded by the church.

Nick Sireau

The church-run Pauluskerk project in Rotterdam cares for hard-drug addicts.

EAST ASIA

Gereja Presbyterian Malaysia (GPM)

Please pray for:

✦ Church planting: for strategic planning and the availability of workers. The GPM's target is to plant 100 churches by the year 2010;

✦ The six Malay speaking congregations which the GPM started several years ago. Pray that competent and godly leaders will emerge from these groups;

✦ The social concern ministries: The Early Intervention Centre teaching children with learning disabilities plans to start drug rehabilitation and a centre for the disabled;

✦ Renewal in worship: young people look for lively, charismatic and contemporary worship;

✦ Young people from the smaller towns studying and working in cities. Pray for the new church in Klang Valley which will cater for the needs of young professionals;

✦ Women pastors and preachers to take on leadership roles in the Synod. Pray for the emergence of more capable, articulate and godly women ministers in the GPM.

The twin towers of Kuala Lumpur.

Presbyterian Church in Taiwan (PCT)

Please pray for:

✦ The Rehabilitation and Care Centres established after the 1999 earthquake;

✦ The 21st Century New Taiwan Mission Movement focusing on spiritual renewal and community action;

✦ Ministries to migrant workers (particularly Filipino and Thai);

✦ The PCT Mass Media Centre;

✦ Justice and peace between Taiwan and China and countries in the Asia-Pacific region;

✦ The restructuring of the PCT General Assembly – from April 2000 the general assembly meeting will be every two years instead of annually.

Presbyterian Church in Singapore (PCS)

Pray for:
✦ The 120th anniversary celebrations: preparations for a worship service in April 2001 for all members;
✦ Plans to build a secondary school in Phomn Pheh, Cambodia;
✦ God's provision for local congregations as they plan to build new churches.

A drop-in centre for the elderly managed by the PCS.

Hong Kong Council of the Church of Christ in China (HKCCCC)

Pray for:
✦ The Building Healthy Churches theme: self-evaluation and long-term development plans for local congregations;
✦ Lay training: the HKCCCC is looking for more staff to participate in lay training;
✦ The renovation of old school buildings.

Presbyterian Church of Korea (PCK)

Pray for:
✦ The leaders of Korea as the economy recovers from the financial crisis;
✦ Just and peaceful communities;
✦ Reconciliation between North and South Korea.

Farmers in Seoul protesting against harsh economic conditions.

PACIFIC

Kiribati Protestant Church (KPC)

Pray:
+ That pastors will be strengthened, and that pastors and congregations will know what real servanthood means in their ministry;
+ For the youth conventions of the northern and southern synods;
+ For the KPC's Theological College, for its upgrading to Bachelor of Divinity level in 2002;
+ For the women's fellowship, youth, evangelism and Sunday school leaders to be strengthened and to know their roles and tasks in their ministry;
+ That KPC members will participate more in worship and bible study.

Nauru Congregational Church (NCC)

Pray for:
+ The future economy of Nauru as the phosphate reserves that were its wealth are nearly exhausted;
+ The Christian Youth Fellowship.

Ekalesia Kelisiano Tuvalu (EKT)

Pray:
+ For the government as it is reviewing the constitution of Tuvalu;
+ That tourists will respect Tuvalu's environment;
+ For women in Tuvalu who seek recognition in traditional communities;
+ For the empowering of youth within the EKT.

Congregational Christian Church in American Samoa (CCCAS)

Please pray:
+ That God will strengthen the CCCAS's ministry;
+ For the government of American Samoa;
+ That the CCCAS will find new ways of expanding and doing mission worldwide.

United Church in Solomon Islands (UCSI)

Please pray for:
+ The training of leaders and lay people for mission;
+ The skills training project for school drop-outs and the unemployed;
+ The church's urban ministry among young people.

United Church in Papua New Guinea (UCPNG)

Please pray:

✦ For the negotiations for a government in post-war Bougainville;

✦ For the church's God Investing in the Family theme, especially for its weekly radio programme which aims to strengthen and build up families;

✦ For the many drug addicts and AIDS patients;

✦ For the UCPNG's finances;

✦ That Papua New Guinea's 800 cultures will co-exist peacefully.

Presbyterian Church of Aotearoa New Zealand (PCANZ)

Pray that:

✦ The growing inequality between rich and poor may be overcome so that indigenous Maori and Pacific island people may share the full benefit of living in Aotearoa New Zealand;

✦ National and regional structures will support congregations through stronger prayer and financial networks;

✦ The church find itself renewed for mission at every level.

Congregational Christian Church in Samoa (CCCS)

Pray for:

✦ CCCS missionaries in the Marshall Islands;

✦ The CCCS pensioners; remember their services for God in the church's mission;

✦ The development of the CCCS's education system;

✦ The establishment of new CCCS congregations in New Zealand, Australia, Hawaii and the US;

✦ The CCCS loan scheme which has become a great help for small congregations.

Congregational Union of New Zealand (CUNZ)

Pray that:

✦ Churches will receive positively the five-year mission programme;

✦ A greater number of teenagers and young adults will develop a deeper commitment for the Lord through the Teens and Young Adults programmes;

✦ Healing will come through the ministries in each of the churches to families who've suffered from child abuse, alcohol and drugs, poverty, spouse neglect, unemployment and despair;

✦ The Gospel is shared with those who are turning from God;

✦ The development of the Auckland Women's Multiracial Fellowship and their outreach will bear much fruit.

SOUTH ASIA

Church of North India (CNI)

Pray for:

✦ Christians persecuted in the state of Gujarat. Pray for those persecuting them. Pray that the God of peace and reconciliation will restore harmony in the area;

✦ The projects run by the Leprosy Mission in India and for those affected by leprosy. Pray for the success of new programmes to tackle the disease and that people with leprosy will be well treated by their communities.

Shona Thangavel

Thousands of young people worshipping God at a CNI rally.

Presbyterian Church of Myanmar (PCM)

Give thanks for the growing churches in Tedim and Zo.

Please pray for:

✦ The evangelists in the remote mission areas;

✦ The relocation of Tahan Theological College to the outskirts of Tahan city;

✦ The Tahan Agape Clinic's staff and patients and their continuing struggles to find equipment and drugs.

Church of Bangladesh (CoB)

Pray for:

✦ The renewal of congregational life;

✦ Sulota Drong, Meya Sarkar and Marina Sarder, the first mission partners with the United Church of Zambia;

✦ Understanding and peace among the nation's political parties;

✦ The Church to reach out to the poor in city and rural areas.

Villagers threshing wheat in Ratanpur.

Church of South India (CSI)

Pray for:

✦ The CSI's Diaconal ministry working for social justice;

✦ The Dalits (untouchables) and Adivasi (tribal) people struggling for their rights;

✦ The youth department to renew the church's youth ministry;

✦ The campaign to stop discrimination against girls in Indian society;

✦ The empowerment of the socially and economically weaker dioceses.

Presbyterian Church of India (PCI)

Please pray for:

✦ The people of North East India who are living under the threat of insurgency and ethnic violence;

✦ The mission workers of the PCI in the two new mission fields at Byrwai and Marngar;

✦ Better understanding and networking between the churches in the region;

✦ More active participation of women in the PCI;

✦ The youth who are hard hit by increasing unemployment;

✦ The Platinum Jubilee Celebrations of the PCI.

Rural life in Mizoram.

AFRICA

United Church of Zambia (UCZ)

Give thanks:
+ For the political stability in Zambia enabling the Gospel to be spread over the past years;
+ For the numerical growth of the UCZ.

Pray for:
+ The parliamentary and presidential elections at the end of 2001;
+ The socio-economic recovery of the country;
+ The leadership of the UCZ from synod to congregations: for determination, perseverance, creativity, innovation and faithfulness;
+ Projects: bee-keeping in Pongwe, women's centres in Lusaka and Kabwe, an orphanage in Ndola, and a new synod office in Lusaka;
+ The newly created eastern presbytery.

Church of Jesus Christ in Madagascar (FJKM)

Give thanks for:
+ The church's development projects, especially in the rural areas;
+ The lay training programme in all regional synods;
+ The extension of Radio Fahazavana, FJKM's radio service.

Pray for:
+ The FJKM's officers at synod, regional and congregational levels to be filled with the Holy Spirit and to be true witnesses of the love of God;
+ The programmes to combat corruption;
+ The literacy programme;
+ The efforts to restore God's creation;
+ The efforts to educate people about hygiene, self respect and human rights.

Sylvia Coombs

Villagers grow soya as part of an FJKM subsistence farming project near Ambositra.

Churches of Christ in Malawi (CCM)

Pray:

✦ For the CCM's evangelism and church planting programme to bring people to Christ in rural areas and cities. Pray for funds and practical needs;

✦ For unity among the CCM congregations and that this will lead to growth in numbers;

✦ That grassroots members will be encouraged to participate in mission.

Michael Heaney

A maize mill at Gowa Mission run by the CCM and funded by CWM.

United Congregational Church of Southern Africa (UCCSA)
(comprising synods in Botswana, Mozambique, Namibia, South Africa and Zimbabwe)

Pray for:
✦ The cancellation of Africa's debt burden;
✦ The alleviation of poverty in the five UCCSA countries;
✦ A cure to AIDS;
✦ A reversal of the moral breakdown of southern Africa;
✦ The renewal of family life within African societies.

Uniting Presbyterian Church in Southern Africa (UPCSA)
(comprising presbyteries in South Africa, Zambia and Zimbabwe)

Give thanks:
✦ For the union of the Presbyterian Church of Southern Africa and the Reformed Presbyterian Church of South Africa, enabling them to strengthen their witness to Jesus Christ and further empower their people in their outreach.

Please pray for:
✦ The first woman moderator, Rev Diane Vorster, as she takes office in 2001;
✦ The churches in Zimbabwe and Zambia, that they will fully participate in UPCSA;
✦ The response of the churches' to the AIDS pandemic;
✦ The control and reduction of violent crime in southern Africa.

CARIBBEAN

United Church in Jamaica and the Cayman Islands (UCJCI)

Please pray:

✦ For the UCJCI as it develops its own style of worship and prayer;

✦ That local congregations will reach out to those in need with the Gospel;

✦ That the UCJCI be even more active in promoting co-operation between denominations;

✦ That the church will encourage ministry that breaks barriers separating people from each other and from God.

Nick Streau

Worship at Elmslie United on Grand Cayman.

Front cover: Children at a UCJCI school near Montego Bay, Jamaica.

Guyana Congregational Union (GCU)

Please pray for:

✦ The successful implementation of the GCU's three-to-five year development programme;

✦ The successful completion of the GCU's second Lay Pastors In-service Certificate Course – Training Programme;

✦ The Youth Arm of the GCU: for spiritual and numerical growth, the accomplishment of their goals for the year, inspiration to deal with the challenges of unemployment and the current economic crisis, and that they build bridges to the older people in their congregations and communities.

Council for World Mission, Ipalo House, 32-34 Great Peter Street, London SW1P 2DB, UK
Tel: +44 (0)20 7222 4214   Fax: +44 (0)20 7233 1747 or +44 (0)20 7222 3510
Email: council@cwmission.org.uk   http://www.cwmission.org.uk   Registered Charity No 232868
Printed by Healeys Printers, Ipswich, UK

Acts 9:36-43   Psalm 23
Revelation 7:9-17
John 10:22-30

Easter 4

I used to wear Ghanaian dress all the time. Now the Ghanaian dress was in three pieces. There was a skirt that was just a long piece of cloth, I guess about five yards wide, and you wrapped it around. It didn't have zippers or anything. And that's one piece. The second was a waist. But the distinctive thing about it was that it had a peplum that extended about five or six inches. This peplum could be pleated or it could be gathered, or it could be just straight. The third piece was a stole. Again it was five yards, just like the skirt. But you could fold it and usually the women would wear it just straight over the shoulder. And if it was cool at night, then you'd use it as a wrap. I had some very beautiful dresses.... I love wearing Ghanaian dresses. And if I would go somewhere, nobody knew that I wasn't Ghanaian, unless I spoke.

Dona Irvin

Preaching at a service for the World Day of Prayer prepared by the women of Ghana, I wore my African clothes; clothes like those worn by many women in Africa. After the service the one black woman in the white congregation came up to me and asked 'Where are you from?'. 'From Britain' I answered. 'You can't be,' she replied. 'I've never seen a white woman wear a black woman's clothes before'. That may be so, but it seems to me that when the sisters grown up together, don't they wear each others' clothes?

Janet Lees

Pray with those engaged in work for racial justice.

71

Read: Revelation 21:1-6

Listen, God,
novelty isn't everything.
What happened to tradition?
Why can't things stay as they are?
Isn't the church meant to be about unchanging things?
Now we have
new people with strange ways
new music we don't know.
The church isn't what it used to be.

> *No.*
> *Nothing is as it used to be*
> *(only Godself, beginning and end of everything).*
> *To live my way you need a new way of thinking,*
> *new dreams, new songs and especially*
> *a new commandment.*
> *Because I am making everything new.*
> *Including you.*

God help me
to embrace your new creation
even if it's not what I'm used to;
to sing your new song
even though I don't know the tune;
and to obey your new commandment
even when I'm afraid to love because I don't understand.
Because (although novelty isn't everything)
I want to be part of your new heaven and new earth
and so I know
I need to be made new.

Acts 11:1-18   Psalm 148
Revelation 21:1-6
John 13:31-35

The Vision of St Peter

St Peter, lying in a hammock
on his brother's verandah,
saw the sky open like a coconut
and a sheet, knit at four corners,
descend towards him. Peering
over the edge, like inquisitive angels,
were goats, monkey, parrots,
toucans, kiskadees, kling-klings,
alligators, iguana, manatees:
the creatures festooned with palm-leaves
and flowers -
bouganvillea, frangipani, poinsettia.

A voice spoke: "Come, knit hands..."

The vision faded. But in his heart
Peter saw the people of his beloved islands
(Antigua, St Vincent, Grenada, Trinidad)
knitted together in love
and swimming free, like fish,
in the starry depths of the Caribbean Sea.

Alan Payne

Pray with partner churches in the Caribbean region of CWM.

God, whose love is without end,
whose purposes are only good,
the story of your people begins in a garden
and ends in a city.
You lead us from primal simplicity
to the peak of human achievement,
from the garden of Eden to the New Jerusalem,
and in your purpose is the hallowing of all we are
and everything we do.

But we have not based our structures
on your designs of justice, peace and love,
we have built monuments to human power,
based on injustice and exploitation.
So our cities are fragmented places
where the rich build security fences
to protect their property from the poor,
and families sleep on the streets.

Forgive us, God of love,
for the parodies of the Holy City which we have built.
Show us how to build communities according to your plan
which places life at the centre of the city
and healing as its first concern,
where there is no need to close anyone out
for everyone is welcome,
where all the variety of human enterprise
and all the splendour of our wealth belongs first to you,
to serve your purposes of love and justice.

Help us in the shabbiness and squalor
to see practical ways of building human cities
which will become, by your grace, the city of God.

Easter 6

The Churches Regeneration Strategy Group (CRSG) is part of South Yorkshire Churches Together for Economic and Social Regeneration. CRSG is central to its work because churches involved in regeneration need to network with each other; those beginning new projects need to network with those who have tried and either succeeded or failed. The experiences of churches in regeneration needs to be fed back into the policy making at local, regional and national level. The aims of CRSG in Sheffield are:

- **to help** churches in each local area to work together on issues of social and economic regeneration by tackling aspects of social exclusion relevant to people in their areas,

- **to become** the body to which the local authority and others refer on matters of social and economic regeneration,

- **to listen** to the difficulties encountered,

- **to prioritise** the work of local regeneration,

- **to share** opportunities and experiences,

- **to network** in a mutually supportive way,

- **to prophecy** as a voice to tackle social exclusion from a Christian perspective,

- **to inform** church leaders and others about our experiences of local regeneration,

- **to find** a common voice to use our experiences to inform regional and national government,

- **to change** and develop according to the demands of local regeneration.

By this we hope to create a new city for all of Sheffield's people.

Janet Lees

Pray for our cities.

Read: **Luke 24:50-53; Psalm 47**

Only the ones who were there
knew what it felt like.
One minute he was there, then gone
up into the sunlit sky,
and our hearts rose with him
so that we soared in spirit
laughing, singing, touching heaven,
and we knew something was ending
and something was beginning
and the ending and the beginning were one.
For God has gone up in triumph.

Great God of heaven and earth and all that is,
you are always with us
and we have grown used to the idea of your nearness
so that we no longer look up in awe and amazement,
recognising in wonder
that you span earth and heaven
in a moment.

As we stand in this moment
and see old plans and projects end,
new ideas and fresh understanding emerge,
help us to make the quantum leap into the new,
and understand that in the vastness of the future
and the solid familiarity of today,
your living loving presence
never ends.

Ascension

Ascension Day in Glasgow

But when he made the final grab, felt the bag in his hand, pushed the old dear over, he was convulsed with pain. He swore at himself; knew the pain wasn't real. Nothing wrong with him, just the acid. Another deep breath. Then he looked around, making sure the city hadn't started disintegrating again. It hadn't, but something else was happening. At first, for a split second, he thought he was rising up off the ground, but the he realised he wasn't. It was the other way round, the earth was falling away beneath him.

The whole country was plunging away from him...The city opened up below him, under his dangling feet. Its towers, its turrets and high-rises paltry and mean from up here, caked in soiled sleet... He found himself facing north-wards towards his old estate. The sight of it woke him from the faint that was engulfing him; its grey concrete lay still and white and shapeless, like mist that had seeped down from the tiny hills behind. It surprised him how close the place was to the rest of the city.

Eventually Morag and Grace had to let go of one another and the vision faded in the mist.
Mother and daughter separated slowly, turning to wave every few seconds, Grace, heading west, via Bunnahabhain Road, Morag, south, down the hill.
Halfway down, the rain came on and the sky darkened. Morag saw people scurrying along the main streets below, putting on hats and pulling on scarves and hoisting umbrellas, all of them glancing up at the threatening March sky, waiting for the heavens to open.

Chris Dolan

Pray with partner churches in the South-east region of England and for those working for regeneration.

Read: Acts 16:16-34

Where the gifts of God are perverted
in the service of greed,
We will affirm your spirit of truth.

Where corrupt traders exploit human beings for profit,
We will affirm your spirit of justice.

Where the forces of justice are swayed by fear of public opinion,
where the innocent are beaten and imprisoned
and there is nothing we can do,
We will find a voice to praise you.

**And when we are singing in the dark
shake us and wake us to your powerful love
which frees and enlightens us all.**

Easter 7

I think of the doctor who suffers depression - a successful, good, highly-regarded Christian. He talks about a 'blanket' coming over him. People say he should snap out of it but there's nothing he can do to lift it off, and he feels compelled to hide the fact that he's on medication for depression. I think of a young woman who committed suicide, drugs were involved, and the underlying concern for the family was one of shame and embarrassment, expressed in a desire for a very private, family-only funeral. You can't expect people to open up then, if there hasn't all the time been an openness about mental health issues.

The only thing I've seen helping is the gospel of love; it's patient, it's not about winning and losing, it's not about good and evil, it's not judging. It embraces all the fuzzy boundaries. The only love big enough is God's love; sometimes it is enough simply to talk of that love.

Resources that are missing are prayers and liturgies that heighten awareness of the complexity of mental illness: it's something that should be named every week because it is with us every week, named in such a way that helps to make it easier for people to speak about these things.

Sue Paterson

Unspoken naming

You will need some thin white candles and some dark coloured water colour paints (browns, greys, purples) and brushes, and some small pieces of card and a tray of sand. In your group use the blunt ends of the candles to write on the card some of your responses to the readings, reflections and prayer for this week. Then place the candles in the sand tray. Try to name some of the unspoken things about mental illness that you know about on your card. Shuffle up the pieces of card and give one to everyone in the group with a paint brush. Paint over the card with some of the water colour paint - you should find that the wax message or word already on the card will appear through the paint. Place the cards around the sand tray, and as each person says the word or message they have uncovered light the candles in the sand tray.

Pray with people released from prison; for the Exodus House project of the Reformed Churches in the Netherlands and any local initiatives known to you.

Read: Acts 2:1-21

It is what anyone might call a risk
strong wind and fire
a dangerous mix
roaring through an upstairs room
full of people.

But here there are no screams of pain
or blazing timbers
no smoke-streaked fire-fighter
with practised eye assessing strength of beam
and length of hose
and likelihood of roof collapse
and screaming death.

Only the joyful sound of sudden laughter
as foreign passers-by hear tones of home
and turning in amazement understand
the marvels God has done for every land.

God of elemental power,
your Spirit shakes our lives!
This wind, this fire
mingle with earth and water to declare
love freed among us,
sweeping through the world
through rooms where people meet
through working hands
and singing voice
and symphony and dance
and every thread of life
risking
explosion
of
eternal joy!

Pentecost

I come from the land of spirits

I come from Korea, the land of spirits full of *Han*. *Han* is anger.
Han is resentment. *Han* is bitterness. *Han* is grief. *Han* is broken-
heartedness and the raw energy for the struggle for liberation.
In my tradition, people who were killed or died unjustly became
wandering spirits, the *Han*-ridden spirits. They are all over the
place, seeking the chance to make the wrong right. Therefore the
living people's responsibility is to listen to the voices of the *Han*-
ridden spirits and to participate in the spirits' work of making right
whatever is wrong.

These *Han*-ridden spirits in our people's history have been the
agents through whom the Holy Spirit has spoken her compassion
and wisdom for life. Without hearing the cries of these spirits, we
cannot hear the voice of the Holy Spirit... They are the icons of the
Holy Spirit who became tangible and visible to us. Because of
them we can feel, touch and taste the concrete bodily historical
presence of the Holy Spirit in our midst...

After many years of infantile prayers, I know there is no magical
solution to human sinfulness and for healing our wounds. I also
know that I no longer believe in an omnipotent, macho, warrior
God who rescues all good guys and punishes all bad guys. Rather,
I rely on the compassionate God who weeps with us for life in the
midst of the cruel destruction of life.

Chung Hyun-Kyung

Pray with partner churches in Korea and Singapore.

Read: **Proverbs 8:1-4,22-31; John 16:12-15; Romans 5:1-5**

God of Wisdom,
when I reach the crossroads and must choose the way,
when I tire on the road and want to stop,
when I stand at the peak and survey new horizons,
or hesitate in the gate of a new place,
let me hear your Wisdom calling playfully
with delight, "Here, here is the way!"

God of Truth,
when I do not know what to believe,
when I need insight and discernment,
when I wonder what is before me,
or cannot make sense of what I see,
let me see your Spirit's guiding flame
lighting my way to truth.

God of Love
when I have to endure hard things,
when I am tested to the limit,
when I am losing hope
or giving in to apathy,
let me be flooded by your love
so that my heart is full of joy.

Wisdom, truth and love
surround me, lead me, inspire me.

> **Do:** **Wait on a street corner for a while, or look out of your door or window onto the street. On some small pieces of paper or post-it notes make a note of what is happening, what you see or hear or smell going on. In a group, or on your own, collect the observations and place them on or around a map, photo or drawing of your local area. Use this as a background as you listen to this week's reading from Proverbs chapter 8.**

Pride House is a small community centre located in an ordinary council house in Eden Hill, Peterlee's most disadvantaged estate. It was originally set up by the police as a community project to help prevent youth disaffection and crime, though it has since branched out into other directions.

A group of local women had become involved in the centre over time, because their children used it for social activities. When planning an outing to the seaside for young people connected with Pride House, the women discovered they would need some formal health and safety and first aid training, which was delivered on a one-off basis by the local college at Pride House itself. The women enjoyed their course so much that it led them all into further learning. Three of them, who before their involvement with the centre had had no qualifications, now have university degrees and still live in Eden Hill.

Skills for Neighbourhood Renewal: Local Solutions

Pray for local initiatives to find wisdom in your neighbourhood, and for partner churches in the East and West Midlands regions of England and for those working for regeneration.

Read: I Kings 21:1-21; Luke 7:36-8:3

Who owns the land?
Some things are not for sale -
my inheritance,
my history,
my identity,
myself.

God of justice, we pray
for people driven off their land
communities destroyed
so that trees can be felled,
the land drilled for minerals,
to put money in the pockets of those who have plenty
at the expense of those who have only themselves
precious and unique.

Who loves the most?
Some things cannot be bought -
my respect
my devotion
my worship
myself.

God of love, we pray
for women abused and exploited
excluded and despised
by those who have used them
and by respectable society,
which turns a blind eye to exploitation
and refuses to speak on behalf of the powerless
who have only love to give.

Teach us to build a community and a world
where everyone is valued justly
and loved freely.

I Kings 21:1-10,(11-14),15-21a
Psalm 5:1-8   Luke 7:36-8:3
Galatians 2:15-21

2 after Pentecost

Falling UK milk prices caused the community of Ampleforth Abbey in North Yorkshire to decide to sell off its herd of dairy cattle in the Spring of 2000. It is estimated that over the past 4 years over 4,000 dairy farms have gone out of production which accounts for 16% of the UK total.

News item from March 2000

Farmers are only getting 15p per litre of milk. This is below cost and is driving the industry to its knees.

Richard Haddock, Farmers for Action

Cheese has been made on the Hebridean Island of Islay for generations. The creamery at Port Charlotte has produced the distinctive mild cheese from the milk of more than 800 cows on the island. However these cows will be sold for slaughter on the mainland and the island will loose at least 300 jobs, for a population of 3,000 people, when the business closes after receivers have been called in due to the slump in dairy farming.

News item from April 2000

In the UK farming families care for 80% of the land and produce about 70% of our food, employing over 600,000 people. However, in recent years farm incomes have fallen by 60% and 18,000 farmers and farm workers lost their jobs in 1999 alone.

Arthur Rank Centre

Pray with farmers and farmworkers and their families.

Read: I Kings 19:1-15a; Luke 8:26-39

Comforting God, we hold before you
all who are alone
hiding away from threats, real or imagined,
paralysed by failure and despair,
depressed, fearful, suicidal.
Let them hear your gentle murmur
coaxing them back to life.

Healing God, we hold before you
isolated people, suffering from mental illness,
shuffling and muttering in city streets,
embarrassing, disgusting us with their antics
so that we hurry away, repelled and ashamed.
Give us the grace to greet them with kindness
and respect, and work for their wellbeing.

Loving God, it is not good for a person to be alone.
Wherever people are working to build communities
that reach out to the lonely and the excluded,
you work with them.
Wherever hands stretch out to embrace the alienated
they are your hands.
Let them also be ours.

.... but the Lord was not in the wind.

God is bigger than the cosmic sadist who took our dearly loved granny away when we were ten. God is bigger than the old man in the sky who is obsessed with sexual conduct, but has no interest in financial misdemeanours. God is bigger than the Protestant deity who blesses the orange sash and despises the rosary. God has moved on from the hymns we sang in childhood. God has moved on from our conversion experience in the Kelvin Hall. God has moved on from the 16th century language of the Authorised Version. God has moved on from the male dominated assemblies that our churches used to be.

And the price to be paid for worshipping such a God is that our ideas of God has always to be changing, always growing bigger.

John Bell

Getting bigger

In your group, or on your own, draw a series of circles on a large piece of paper; a small one in the middle, gradually getting larger to the edge of the paper. Ask people to suggest images and ideas about God which they recall from their earliest memories and put these in the inner circle. Then recall other ideas and images about God from other periods of life and put these in the subsequent circles. Refer to hymns and prayers people use or have used as a source for these ideas and images if memory dries up. Conclude your time together by saying or singing a version of Psalm 42.

Pray with partner churches in Malaysia and their drug rehabilitation work.

Life in the Spirit

Read: Galatians 5:1,13-25

Renewing Spirit,
enter our lives with your energy and vitality,
fill us once again with your presence,
renew in us our faith and witness,
that we may give praise and thanksgiving to our God.

Holy Spirit, source of our life, flow within us.

Resourcing Spirit,
empty us to receive your harvest,
challenge us to accept the gift we have received,
enable us to share that harvest with others
that Christ may be known through us.

Holy Spirit, source of our life, flow within us.

Guiding Spirit,
free us from gossip and infighting in our communities,
lead us from self-indulgence to generosity in our actions,
grant us grace not to be conceited or envious of one another
that we may become citizens of God's Kingdom.

Holy Spirit, source of our life, flow within us.

2 Kings 2:1-2, 6-14
Psalm 77:1-2, 11-20
Galatians 5:1, 13-25   Luke 9:51-62

after Pentecost

Homes for worms

I have been representing the thousands of worms working on a voluntary basis at RECYC [a Sheffield based recycling initiative] for quite some time now. Barry had raised us telling us that we could benefit greatly in months to come by working co-operatively and keeping quiet. This suited our interests so much that our commitment was 100 percent. New homes were provided and the food never stopped coming. Our young were sold by the hundreds to loving families who were busy refurbishing their own compost homes and wanted to enjoy the new tenants.... We are surprised that compost homes of any sort are not more readily available. Looking ahead the future for us worms seems full of promise. For how many years have we sadly watched tones and tones of food which would rightfully be ours removed and treated as *waste*? And we can eat a considerable range of food I can tell you... Our day will come.

Walter Worm

Should you be giving some worms a home or getting involved in local recycling initiatives? Still not looked at *'Roots and Branches'* (material for churches on ecological issues)? Still not used the bottle bank or made any compost? Just what are you doing with your life, and the life of the planet?

Pray for local recycling initiatives and churches working on ecological projects.

89

Read: 2 Kings 5:1-14

Healing God,
in the knitting of bones,
in the growth of new tissue,
in the building of muscle,
you are there.

Healing God,
in the lifting of despair,
in the silencing of fear,
in the acceptance of memories,
you are there.

Healing God,
in the reconciliation of former adversaries,
in each movement towards justice
in the search for life amidst death,
you are there.

Healing God,
take each one of us as we are,
battered and bruised by life's experiences,
restore within us a sense of your peace,
that we may find healing.

2 Kings 5:1-14   Psalm 30
Galatians 6: (1-6) 7-16
Luke 10:1-11, 16-20

5 after Pentecost

Healing the local community

Pie in the Sky cafe is a self-financing community business which employs 6 people. The cafe has become popular with staff, local people and those working in the area. It undertakes outside catering offering high quality food at competitive prices.

The Health Project aims to promote the health of the residents of Bromley by Bow by the provision of community and clinical services, offering an integrated, holistic approach to health in its widest sense.

The Community Care Project is a major day care provider to people assessed by Social Services as having high priority care needs. We have developed a model of care quite unique in this area which combines day-care with a community development approach. Local volunteers work on a one to one basis with people who have a disability or particular care needs and relationships are built on mutual trust and friendship. In return, volunteers are offered training opportunities, social support in life and the chance to do an NVQ qualification in Developmental Care.

Bromley By Bow Church is the heart of the Centre both physically and psychologically. The liturgical space remains a core sanctuary around which the bustle of the day revolves. Like the mediaeval Cathedral, the church sits amidst the market place of everyday activities, allowing the vibrancy and diversity of life to surround it. The church continues to be a living place of worship within the Centre, offering a place for prayer and reflection and has a commitment to finding new ways of bringing people together.

Bromley By Bow Centre

Pray with partner churches working for healing in communities and health initiatives.

Read: Colossians 1:13-14

Sung response from Taize community.
**'The Lord is my light, my light and my salvation.
In God I trust, in God I trust.'**

Holy God,
your light shines into the darkness,
overcoming it, banishing it from your presence,
flooding everything with your glory.
From the darkness you lead us into the
light of your kingdom.

**The Lord is my light, my light and my salvation.
In God I trust, in God I trust.**

Holy God,
in giving us your son
you release us from darkness.
You bring us into a new relationship with you.
From the darkness you lead us
to call you Abba, Father.

**The Lord is my light, my light and my salvation.
In God I trust, in God I trust.**

Holy God,
you offer us forgiveness for our sins,
you hold out open hands of reconciliation,
you rescue us to be the people you would have us be.
From the darkness you lead us into
the promise of new life.

**The Lord is my light, my light and my salvation.
In God I trust, in God I trust.**

A local by-election demonstrated the rise in popular support for the British National Party. One of the clergy described the community voting in a member of the BNP at a council by-election as a riot via the ballot box.

The myth that had gained currency was that most of the new, affordable social housing was being allocated to Bangladeshi families. The church leaders instigated research which demonstrated that this was not the case, and church members and others were recruited to distribute this information throughout the community. With the exception of the children, very few white or Afro-Caribbean people knew any Bangladeshis. So a New Year party was organised and thirty Bangladeshi people attended, along with forty others. The party started with everyone standing on a giant map of the Isle of Dogs to represent where they lived and who was a neighbour to whom.

In the days running up to [the next] elections people were invited to wear 'rainbow' ribbons to publicly demonstrate their commitment to a racially diverse Isle of Dogs. Church members were thus challenged to decide which side of the fence they were on. It was a time of testing for church members. For church members the tension between solidarity and betrayal was more painful than it was for church leaders. Others, particularly those outside the church, were quick to comment that the churches were being too political and too 'pro-Asian'. To become 'cosmopolitan' would be to betray one's peers, and to enter into solidarity with those at the bottom of the pile opened people to ostracism by their long-standing neighbours.   *Ann Morisy*

Have a party

Have a party for local people. This party should not be for the people who already come to your church nor even for the neighbours those people already know. It should be for those 'at the bottom of the pile', the people that are the subject of local gossip, hate or mistrust. Like the people at the Isle of Dogs try to find out who lives near to who, and discover some new neighbours. It need not be an expensive party. Ask all that agree to come to make something to bring - food, drink, entertainment.

Pray with partner churches in the Solomon Islands and in Papua New Guinea.

Merciful God,
too often we forget to rely upon you,
we reject your faithful love
and fall back on our own strengths and initiatives.

Forgive us when we are filled with pride at another's expense,
when we put others down for our own benefit,
when our words and thoughts are unkind, or untruthful.

Forgive us when we rush past the Big Issue seller on the street,
and gaze intently at the pavement as we pass by beggars,
when we ignore the volunteer rattling the charity can at the
supermarket.

Forgive us when we pay lip service to our faith so we can
'get on with life',
when we are caught up in the commercialisation of Christmas,
and we forget that shopworkers also need a day of re-creation.

Merciful God, you choose to forgive
rather than punish us when we rely upon ourselves.
Thank you for continually giving us another chance.
Thank you for your faithful love.

I get angry about sermons that offer an interpretation of Luke 10:38-42 that is against Martha, or against them both and thereby against us as women. I've certainly heard it quite often: once at a dysfunctional ageing almost all white Synod meeting. Martha's too busy and shouldn't be and Mary is right to stay silent. What a great pair of role models they make! No wonder they are trotted out to faithful Christian women so often. Forget it. What we need is liberation and so do they. Let's go to Bethany and listen to the silence in this story and see what we find. Read it alongside all we know, and much more we don't, about this family, adding what we know from our experiences of life in families of all sorts. Martha, Mary and Lazarus live together; the first sign that this family did not conform to social norms: three adult siblings living together under one roof - unheard of in a society in which adults all married. I say all, because the only ones that didn't would be the impaired ones, the marginalised ones, the ones not quite able to function socially. John (chapter 11) gives us a clue when he says that the crowd at the tomb wondered why Jesus, who could cure the blind person, could not have saved Lazarus. The blind people in the gospels have in common that they were amongst the most marginal in that society: living by begging or by relying on their family. Lazarus lived with his unmarried sisters and is likened by the crowd to the blind person. It might be reasonable to assume that Lazarus was in some way disabled. Whatever it was, it was not talked about.

Mary says little, which Luke commends. She finds help to bear family burdens in Jesus company, while Martha copes by getting on with trying to make a home for everyone. We all cope differently; there's no need to read the story against one sister or the other. And I don't believe Jesus does that. If he would like Martha to face up to the reality of the situation then he leaves her to do it in her own way in her own time which she does. After Lazarus' death she talks with him alone saying 'If you'd been here my brother would not have died - but I know you are the Life Giver - for all my clattering about in the kitchen I know that too'. And he confirms her faith there and then: Martha becomes visible.

Mary breaks her silence after Lazarus' death. Perhaps she speaks only occasionally because she is an elective mute. That's how she copes in this family, by choosing silence. Jesus never reprimands her for that. Silence is not a bad thing. You can choose it if it helps but the Life-Giver also offers other choices. Jesus is the Life-Giver for this family. He hears Martha and affirms her. He hears Mary and affirms her. He calls Lazarus out of the silent tomb. He hears us and affirms us in or out of silence.

Janet Lees

Pray with **partner churches in Hong Kong and for the 'Building healthy churches' scheme.**

Read: Luke 11:9-13

Generous God,
you give so much to us,
yet we have difficulty
in receiving from you.

True receiving asks us
to make ourselves vulnerable,
to open ourselves up,
to give control over to another.

Instead we prefer
to put barriers around ourselves,
to close ranks,
to control what we share with others.

Generous God, teach us to receive,
open our eyes to your vision,
empower us by your Spirit
so that we may fully receive your blessing.

Read: Psalm 85

De Profundis

A time there was -
when no one knew.
When we were not seen,
save a "crime" or scandal.

At time there was -
when we were hated.
When a pink triangle marked us,
and the unmarked grave in Auschwitz beckoned.

A time there is -
when we are attacked:
When nails pierce our flesh,
and Bibles are used as baseball bats.

A time there is-
when we are ignored:
when we are asked to wait,
and we are less important than others who are despised
and rejected:

How long, how long,
O God.

Peter Colwell
written on 30th April 1999 following a bomb attack
on the gay pub 'The Admiral Duncan' in Soho, London

Pray with partner churches in the UK.

Read: Hosea 11:1-4; 8-9.

Mum! Dad! Where are you?

I'm here. Where have you been?
What have you been doing?

Parent God, we've been distracted, tempted, torn away.
We're faithful to you, we're here worshipping you,
but through the week, there's so many others things....

What about your community?

Surviving - often getting through the day
with a cup of dark coffee, a cigarette,
a stiff drink, even a hard drug.

What about the lonely ones?

Searching for soul mates, someone to talk to.
Some escape their isolation through the world wide web,
in the shopping centre, on a chatline, through a dating agency.

What about fear and insecurity?

Simmering below the surface, seeking expression...
I suppose we often hide behind aggressive behaviour,
prejudice, racism,
desperately seek simple answers to complicated questions.

Where are you?

We're lost parent God
lost and very lonely
Help us. Hold us. Heal us.
for only you can find us.

South Skye is a vibrant area where there have been many imaginative developments in recent years. Several new ventures are capitalising on the natural environment and the area's reputation as the 'Garden of Skye'.

Chris Marsh, who runs a company providing a range of woodland consultancy and tree surgery services, was assisted with a £3,000 development grant to diversify into horticulture. His new venture will produce a range of organic fruit and vegetables for local markets and for the emergent vegetable distribution co-operative.

At community level too, the area's cultural heritage is receiving support. Comunn Eachdraidh Shleite (Sleat Local History Society) has been assisted through a Community Action Grant to buy a camcorder to record interviews with the old residents of the Sleat area and visit the historic sites. This type of project preserves the unique heritage of the area and will encourage important interactions between the old and young within the community.

Skye and Lochalsh Enterprise Annual Report 1998/9

Pray with partner churches in the Pacific region of CWM.

Read: Isaiah 1:11-16; Luke 12:32-34

Patient God
We've forgotten how special we are to you.
We spend too long trying to grab your attention
instead of responding to your deep love for us.

We treat our worship as a weekly ritual -
fail to connect it with our work and daily life.

Our sacrifices of praise
and wordy prayers
must weary you;
must weaken your resolve to choose us
and use us
in your work of mission.

How amazing that you don't give up on us,
that we remain special to you
despite our missing the point, again and again,
of your Good News stories.

Show us again, Patient God,
through those who have remained faithful to you
what we can do and be
when we live your kindness
do your justice
throw away our wasted words
and wake up to love in action.

By faith.....

Any woman who gave birth to a square-headed child knew at once
what was expected of her. She, who's place was among the Ordinary
Ones, had to prepare the child for a place among the Wise Ones.
The Wise Ones had their own small territory on a hilltop in the middle
of the tribal lands. They cultivated potatoes, their only crop.
The Ordinary Ones kept asking if it would not be a good thing if they
too tried to cultivate potatoes, for the grain they usually harvested
produced such a poor return that the tribe was chronically
malnourished. The Wise Ones would shake their heads and say
their analysis of the soil showed it to be unsuitable for potatoes.
What was more, they themselves were suffering from diminishing
returns on their potato crop; they could not afford seed for an
experiment. It was better to leave things as they were for one more
year. And so the years went by.
But a woman called Promethea paid a rare visit to her square-headed
daughter. She left four potatoes and instructed her mother how to
prepare and cook them. She rushed away before her mother could
tell her that she had a small bread roll in her bag. Curious about the
potatoes she put them in the bag where the roll had been and
brought them home with her.
She planted the potatoes in her garden and she harvested a bumper
crop. It turned out that there were minerals in the soil which were
particularly suited for potato crops. She gave some to her friends
and they also yielded a good crop. In time the Wise Ones realised
what had happened and came to discuss the development.
This time the Ordinary Ones felt more confident. Their success in
growing potatoes was there for all to see. Finally the Wise Ones
admitted that they had formed too closed a community. In the old
days, almost forgotten, they had been part of the tribe. So the Wise
Ones became wise. The Ordinary Ones showed how extraordinary
is the ordinary. They were nourished together as they never had been
when they lived apart from one another. The community throve on its
new unity.

Ian Fraser

Pray with partner churches in India.

Read: Isaiah 5:1-7; Luke 12:51; Hebrews 12:1-2

I wish you'd give us a break, God...
We're only human.
We're growing the best we can
but we can't always grow sweet -
we don't always feel sweet!
We grow within these walls
to be protected
from a sour world.

I wish you'd stop calling us, God...
with your challenging words:
"Why are you no different from the world
you protect yourselves against?"
"Why keep the walls" you say
"if their protection makes no difference
to the fruit I would know you by
in a world gone wild?".

I wish you'd give us a shake, God...
so that our walls fall down
and we become exposed
to your cloud of witnesses.
We might throw off our wild and world-like ways
if we were forced to grow a little closer
to the "thorns in our (sour) flesh".
Then, growing up, we'd be a better crop.

You're frightened of him when you do the things he wants.
You're frightened of him when you do the things he doesn't want.
What do YOU want to do.

Women have to be able to participate fully in their country's plans,
policies and programmes if development is to take place. As long
as they are stifled in their participation by fear of violence, as long
as they are reluctant to take up leadership positions because they
are subject to physical or emotional abuse, the progress of the
whole population will suffer.
At one theological college in India, young men being trained for the
ministry claimed their 'cultural right' to beat their wives! There was
also the case of the Indian lay preacher who left his young wife
and child to go to Africa to do 'the Lord's work'. A few months
later, he wrote expressing deep concern because he would have to
desert her. God had spoken to him and asked him to marry a
woman who worked with him.

Aruna Gnanadason

Violence is promoted by greed for power and money, desire to
dominate and control others. It is easy to identify with the violence
committed during civil wars and against nature... But I want us to
challenge ourselves on the violence and wars that begin right in
our bedrooms.

Nyambura Njoroge

Pray with organisations supporting survivors of violence and abuse.

When I was born
and first drew breath,
my cries brought smiles of happiness.
New life, all was well,
God's gift faithfully delivered:
my hunger satisfied
my dependency assumed.

When I was born-again
and first knew Jesus for myself,
my commitment brought smiles of satisfaction.
Life in Christ, all felt well,
God's call faithfully answered:
my hunger spirit-filled
my dependency enjoyed.

When I was reborn
and understood the length and breadth of service,
my lack of depth brought smiles of disbelief.
My whole life? All was unwell,
God's calling misdirected:
my hunger still for learning
my dependency elsewhere.

When "Yes!" was born
I understood, my God, the journey was with You.
You matched my fear with smiles of expectation.
Full Life! All will be well,
all things will be well:
You filled my hunger
accepted my dependency.

Plastic power

Grahamstown is a very impoverished community and unemployment is rife. For many people the soup and bread they receive at the soup kitchens administered by the Masithandane Association is their only daily meal. In return for this meal, they are asked to collect used plastic bags and hand them in at the kitchens. This has a two-fold purpose - it helps combat the litter problem, and provides the Masithandane women with the material they need for the plastic hats, bags and mats they make.

The Masithandane Association owes much of its success to plastic bags. Once the women had mastered the craft of turning these bags into useful, saleable items which found a ready market - particularly among tourists who were fascinated by the story behind the project - they were encouraged to revive many of their traditional skills. Soon their beadwork proved to be as popular as their plastic items, and the women began to wear their traditional costumes with pride.

Masithandane Association

Pray with partner churches in South Africa.

Read: Jeremiah 2:4-13; Luke 14:1,7-14

With my computer game, God,
I'm in the action;
zapping the baddies,
saving the planet.
It's amazing, it's addictive,
as I climb the levels and make a place for myself
I feel I've achieved something.

Help me not to be stroppy when the game is over.
Help me enjoy doing the everyday things too.

With the stories of the bible, God,
I'm reading about your action;
plaguing the Egyptians,
till they let your people go.
I'd like a strategy game,
be interactive, join you and Moses
and make that great escape.

Help me to see it's more than just an old story.
Help me log into what you're doing now.

With the world the way it is, God,
We'll have to take some action;
sort out the bullies,
stop people fighting wars.
I'd like to help somehow,
get involved, join up with Jesus
try to change the world.

Help me when all these things don't seem so cool.
Help me to reach the levels of living you want.

At a meeting for industrialist and educationalists in Sefton a discussion started on the problem of "Disaffected Youth". The analysis focused on the fact that even as early as 11 years of age up to 20% of children were opting out of the educational system and, as a consequence, giving up hope of a "normal" job. These children could see no future in the formal employment market and ended up working in the informal economy or the criminal economy.

I asked about the honesty of our description "disaffected", and pointed out that the informal economy:

- is highly deregulated, which, we have been told repeatedly over the last decade, is very desirable,
- is very individualised; also a major trend and apparently a "good thing",
- offers maximum flexibility with people readily switching between types of work; just what we need today,
- is not troubled by Trade Unions, who are seen as a "bad thing",
- is a perfect model of tax free employment.

In other words, what I was saying was:

in as much as they have gone down the road promoted by the government we voted in, it looks as if these young people have got it right, which rather makes the rest of us "disaffected". Is it really honest to go along with the promotion of certain attributes in the economy and then, when they appear, call it "disaffection"? All the dishonest double-speak in this example results in those people already forced into the margins of the economy being labelled "disaffected" which is literal jargon for outsiders, no-marks, people who don't belong, people who are not part of "us". A triple violence is being committed: we push them out of the economy; we identify them as outsiders; and we use language which implies that they themselves made some sort of choice to become "disaffected". The Church cannot sit by and pretend that such a violence is not being done. Where those made in God's image are cheated and slandered the Church has to stand with the victims as they challenge the cheats and liars.

Paul Skirrow

Pray with those working in information technology and related industries.

Out of shape

Do: **Get your hands in some clay**
(air hardening clay is available in most craft shops)

Cups and mugs, plates, cereal bowls,
dishes and jugs, all made in millions...
imperfect ones are thrown away
or sold off cheap as rejects.
It's only the holiday, handicraft shop
or joining the pottery class
that can really help us understand
the way God shapes us.

Retail stores, burger bars, clothes shops,
toys and branded goods, all just the same...
their prices fixed, no copies allowed
to undermine the profit.
But only if we see the crowded sweat shop,
children slaves on poverty wages,
small food producers going broke,
can we understand God's anger.

A lower wage, a faster job, and longer hours,
flexible working, short term contracts, all the way
that global profit is increased
investment doubled, growth improved.
But if we know the unemployed, the overworked,
the families that break with stress
and see the rich exclude the poor
we'll understand we're out of shape.

Creative God
When national pride and global interests
ignore the uniqueness of your handiwork,
take us and return us
make us into something better.

Jeremiah 18:1-11
Psalm 139:1-6,13-18
Philemon 1-21   Luke 14:25-33

14 after Pentecost

I live in an area of holidays and tourism, urban and rural, where shops are full of "tacky" gifts and seconds shops. Where the buzz of the seaside streets contrast with the quieter rural places where handicraft shops can still display traditional skills.

I also live in a world where fast food, warehouse shopping and designer labels win over the young and make them into consumers who demand spending rights from pressurised parents, already guilty enough about their low incomes and inability to match the exciting material world promoters display to their kids. I feel our culture is getting bent out of shape! This prayer reflects all the things that are thrown at us - hinting at choices that either don't exist or have no real meaning and a piling in of all the things which are overtaking us.

Chris Warner

"We take from pottery what we need and give what we can. The incoherent can express themselves vividly through clay; the voluble learn something of silence; and the tense relax. It's all very therapeutic and fulfilling".

Rosemary Varney

Surprised by Joy

As an artist, what I found initially irresistible about Christianity was this all-consuming fire, a love as strong as death... I worried that becoming a Christian would mean the end of creativity, that I would lose the pagan instincts that fire the imagination and the primitive urges to heights of creative power in art, poetry and music.... But, in relenting to the stark gospel of the Cross, I was surprised by the joyful relief of divine humour and knew the absolute futility of the devil's lies. My art didn't perish; I only stopped being a "mere" artist. To be converted to faith is to step into a realm of paradoxes and take on an even more relentless engagement with life, too intense even for art...

I love to think of clay as the most important metaphor for artistic creation. It is a very sensuous medium - soft, obedient and pleasurable to the touch. The artist is in most immediate contact with it, working directly with hands and body. I derive almost childlike delight working in this medium, remembering the time in childhood when playing with dirt and mud was such a grievous misdeed. Clay is a natural plaything and touching it revives old instincts. The thing is to let them out as fast as I can, spontaneously and joyously.

Julie Luch

As the UK summer holiday season comes to an end, pray with those who work in the tourist industry, particularly seasonal workers; for the South-west region of England and its regeneration.

109

Foolish people, fragile world; forgiving God?

Do you still think we're foolish, God,
consumer powered and advert led,
not seeing cost and consequence
nor understanding waste and debt?

While we still "shop until we drop",
in comfort, style, and heated streets,
or internet our orders through
computers to some virtual shop,
and eat and drink crops others cashed
to pay their countries' rising debts,
and purchase toys that children made
deprived of learning or of play.

Do you now think of judgement, God,
against our all consuming greed,
when we well know the cost and still
take what we think we need?

While economic chaos reigns
and hungry people work as slaves,
and light pollution dulls the skies,
and mountains rot from acid rain,
and deserts form where earth is raped:
its trees ripped out, its topsoil lost,
and creatures robbed of habitat,
and seas and shores are hurt and spoiled.

Can you still find the patience, God,
for those caught in this foolish race
and will you help us stop to count
the value of your foolish grace?

Mapping (and rapping) for Mission

When I came to Great Yarmouth over six years ago there was no tradition
of industrial mission here, and many who heard of my move questioned
whether there was any industry here either! Great Yarmouth, like
Blackpool, is known as a holiday resort and for not much else, but it is in
fact a place of considerable diversity: a port town, support base for the
offshore industry in the southern North Sea, an agricultural borough with
food processing industries, a centre for several electronics companies,
retailing, all the usual public sector employers, and all this in addition to
a tourism industry that probably employs the equivalent of around 9,000
full time jobs.

You couldn't blame people for not knowing all this - even the local
population sometimes needs to be reminded of the diversity and
creativity that exists on their doorstep. Businesses in Great Yarmouth are
amazingly good at coming up with unique solutions, whether it be to
build a small boat for island hopping in the South Pacific, inventing a new
style safety helmet for hot weather locations...., and (not known by many)
the famous fish finger.

But set against all this are statistics of the highest unemployment in
Norfolk, the second most deprived travel-to-work area in England, skills
shortages, East Coast isolation and an average income which is half the
national average.

The challenge for industrial mission is to make sense of all the diversity,
activity and exclusion: to encourage the churches to a deeper
understanding of where they fit into this dynamic, despairing scene.

Chris Warner

On your doorstep

What is the diversity of your local area and what are the
challenges? How does your congregation reflect that diversity
and those challenges? At the church meeting, take two different
coloured post-it notes to represent diversity and challenges.
Stick these on a poster of a series of steps (perhaps there are
some outside or inside your church your could use). Plan to
celebrate the diversity and meet some of the challenges over the
next few months. Think of some of the steps you will need to
take to do this. At the next meeting revisit the 'steps' and see
how your understanding has changed.

---

*Pray for the East Anglia region of England and for those working for
regeneration.*

Read: Jeremiah 8:18-9:1; Luke 16:1-13

What are we going to do?
The game's up!
We thought we were kidding you God
but we've been kidding ourselves.
All this squandering of divine creativity
couldn't go unnoticed,
and the world's weeping
is turning into righteous indignation.

We'd better use the wealth we've gained
to make a difference:
release nations from their debts
invest in fairly traded goods
persuade "the market" to pay its debt
for earth's resources
human labour
damaged communities and undisposed of waste.

We've made a start, redeeming God
admittedly with some self interest.
Can you transform that tiny hint of trust
into a hopeful sign of growing up?

16 after Pentecost

Read: Luke 16:1-13

Interviewer: On Special Report Tonight we have an interview with that Steward who featured in the Parable Jesus told yesterday. In view of the adverse publicity he has attracted he has asked to remain anonymous. Now then Mr Steward, you say that your motives in acting as you did were only good ones, but can you explain how you can justify your criminal behaviour?

Steward: Surely you must be able to see that the man I was working for was a greater criminal than me. He has been cheating people for years. There were dozens of people in debt to him, some right over their heads. He would cream off a huge percentage of a man's olive harvest or barley harvest. He would make what looked like favourable advances in lean years only to claw even more back in good years. This kind of behaviour is not condemned even though it makes many families go to the wall, to a debtor's prison and accounts for a high suicide rate, in my view. But when I try to act to reverse this injustice by writing off some of those debts, even if clearly in my own self interest, I'm the criminal.

Interviewer: Are you saying that your employer was not an honest man?

Steward: How could he be if he was as rich as that. You've not seen the books but I know what kind of interest he was charging. He got that rich on the backs of the poor. I have no sympathy for him.

Interviewer: You seem to have stirred up a lot of trouble for yourself. More people seem to support him than support you.

Steward: You mean more rich people like him support him than support me. Only those whose debts I eased support me. I can't expect the rich to agree with what I did. The rich voices are always the loudest.

Interviewer: So what do you make of this Jesus and his use of your story?

Steward: He's right to say you can't serve two masters. It's hard sometimes to serve even one; to compromise yourself for a dishonest man even if he pays your wages. I wrestled with the situation and eventually I had to choose. Writing off the debts of the others, well, I can't claim it was without self interest, but it was also the right thing to do. They deserved better treatment. As for hitting the headlines well, people will soon forget about me. They'll retell the story to suit themselves whether they are rich or poor. I'll soon be forgotten.

Janet Lees

Pray with partner churches in Zambia.

Read: **Jeremiah 32:6-15; Luke 16:19-31; I Timothy 6:6-19**

"Confessions of faith which do not have as their consequence far-reaching social changes in this world, are matters of private recreation, and therefore have long been tolerated as irrelevant and harmless."

Helmut Gollwitzer

We want to grasp The Life, living God.
Not the life of contented religion
and comfortable confessions:
leisure-time loyalty,
free-time faith,
unconnected communities.

We want others to have The Life you promise too.
Not a life enslaved on streets
with unheard stories:
locked in poverty,
full-time seeking survival,
crippled communities.

Help us seek solutions to enslavement:
so that people are free to live and breath,
buy and sell, live securely
in a house that is home.

Lead us wise God
in the ways of justice, piety, integrity, love,
fortitude and gentleness.
For in these are The Life:
Life in its fullness.

Jeremiah 32:1-3a,6-15
Psalm 91:1-6,14-16
I Timothy 6 6-19   Luke 16:19-31

17 after Pentecost

A fundamental Gospel task is to ask the "why" questions, from the edge with those who are on the margins. It is not a Gospel task to be at the centre, delivering ideologically motivated programmes which do not ask the "why" questions at all, and only the "how" questions in an atomised and isolated way. We cannot just take a pragmatic stance.

Paul Skirrow

Between us and them,
between us and the million
named Lazarus,
a great chasm has been fixed:
and we would almost thank you,
almost thank you for our security,
our stout walls,
that we can wind our car windows up
when we're away from home…..
… except for the ache
inside us.
For between us and you, Jesus,
lies the same chasm,
and we are sorry.
We shut the window, Spirit,
against you,
and we are sorry.
We would rather believe, Creator,
that you made Grasmere,
but not Bermondsey,
and we are sorry.
Forgive us God.

We thank you that the hand reaching across the chasm is yours.

Bob Warwicker

Pray with partner churches in Jamaica and the Cayman Islands.

115

Read: **Habakkuk 1:1-4, 2:1-4**

God, it's a war zone
people are beaten up
shot at, murdered in the streets
and you do nothing to stop it.

People disappear
and are found in mass graves
broken and mutilated,
and there is no justice.

God of peace, this is a place of terror;
God of love, this is a time of hate.

We pray today for war correspondents
who stand at the flashpoints of the world
and look for the truth.
Give them clear vision
and help them to be faithful in recording what they see
so that those who hold your vision of justice and peace
may work and wait for it to be real
in every war zone which is also GodZone
God's own.

Legacy

Ten year old Chien was born without legs but after corrective surgery he was fitted with two Jaipur artificial limbs. He will need regular refits and perhaps more surgery as he grows. The war in Vietnam ended over 25 years ago but the scars remain and the effects are felt every day. Nearly every week there are incidents of bomb or mine explosions which kill and maim people. In Quang Tri province, on the 17th Parallel, a monthly report from one hospital alone showed that nearly every day six people needed help with injuries. That makes 2,000 people per year who have been injured by bombs and mines left over from war in just one area.

Estimates vary as to the number of landmines and other unexploded ordinances that remain hidden. Apart from bombs and other weapons, the US forces used Agent Orange, a powerful defoliant which destroyed trees and vegetation and left bare millions of acres of land. This poison is still in the soil and water and causes illnesses and birth defects and disabilities. The work of the Jaipur limb fitting programme in Vietnam is expanding to help rehabilitate some of the thousands of amputees.

Of the many dangers children in Laos face these days, playing with an orange would seem to be one of the lesser ones. However, the bomb live unit 24 looks like an orange and will kill a child if it explodes at close range. There are seven bomblets for every man, woman and child in Vietnam, Cambodia and Laos. Twenty-nine per cent of all victims are children who cause them to detonate by playing with them or by stepping on them accidentally. The children of Laos pay a high price for a war which ended a quarter of a century ago.

Jaipur Limb Campaign

Pray with those working in war zones around the world.

Speaking freely

Read: 2 Kings 5:1-15; 2 Timothy 2:8-10

God we thank you that your word is not chained
but spoken freely by a slave,
sent at second hand by a discourteous prophet,
offered with care and kindness by a servant.

Give us wisdom to hear your word
when it sounds like fantasy or nonsense,
or offends our sense of our own dignity.

Give us love and courage to speak your word
even when it may be dismissed as foolishness
or when it is risky to speak out,

Because you teach us that ordinary people
can speak to the powerful
with your words.

Doing something difficult

Adults do NOT wish to enter a building where they have to fight their way through young people smoking on the steps. The venue (for a learning centre) could be a pub, community centre, cafe, health centre or anywhere they feel comfortable entering and as unlike a school as possible. Many adults have a very poor experience of school and fear failure. The trainers need to appreciate the hopes and fears of the group and be able to empathise with them. Perhaps the first stage of any programme should be to identify and train trainers from that community.

One of the first skills to encourage people to develop is self-belief and self-respect. For people who may not have done well academically it is important that they are able to recognise and articulate those skills that they have developed throughout their lives. Once they realise that they do indeed have very valuable skills, they may well see the relevance to their lives of acquiring some more.

Skills for Neighbourhood Renewal

Pray with partner churches in the East Asia region of CWM.

RULE THE WORLD?
NO I JUST WANT TO
GET AN EDUCATION

Struggle

Powerful God,
you struggle with us
and against us
so that we may be changed
into people whom you have named,
who have seen you face to face.

We pray for all who struggle for justice
in the face of unjust powers.
Give them strength to persist in their demands
and make the powerful act for them.

We pray for people who exercise power
in the face of intractable problems.
Give them ears to hear the cry of the powerless,
and wisdom and courage to govern justly.

God of the struggle,
give to us all
persistence and perception,
courage and strength,
and faith when justice is a long time coming.

Powerful God
you struggle with us
and against us
so that we may be changed
into people whom you have named
who have seen you face to face.

20 after Pentecost
One World Week

Luke 18:1-8

Faces of Scotland

As I begin to tire, my enthusiasm for the journey wanes. This last leg of the trip is a slog. The scenery is now washing over me.....
I took my passenger's word for it that the scenery was, indeed, spectacular. I didn't see any of it. My mouth dry, my eyes frozen on the road ahead, the car stuck firmly in first or second gear, we climbed the twisting seven-mile road through a wall of mountains. My relief at reaching Glenelg was short-lived. Crossing on the ferry I lifted mine eyes unto the hills and saw that once I reached the other side, a trek over similar - if not worse- terrain awaited....
The vastness of Skye always takes me by surprise. The road from Kyleakin to my final destination feels long and weary.

Passing Duntulm Castle, I remember that it was near here in 1979 that Sir Roddy was walking his dog and watching a huge crude oil tanker negotiating the Minch when he realised that the area was staring potential disaster in the face. As he was later to tell me, though you would not know by looking at it, the Minch has treacherous rocks lurking beneath the waves which leave only two spaces through which tankers can pass. These monstrous ships have a turning circle of three-quarters of a mile and they take miles to stop. Any mistake causing a rip in a hull would be a catastrophe not just for Skye and the Outer Hebrides, but for the whole of the west coast of Scotland. Eventually he succeeded in getting charts to show a recommended route for tankers over a certain tonnage which goes around the outside of the Hebrides.

Fiona MacDonald

Pray for **people working in local, regional and national government.**

28 October

Helpless God

Excluded God,
when there is nowhere where you are welcome
no-one to come to your aid,
we who bear your name will surround you.

Stay with us, God,
be our guest,
be our host.

We will protect you,
vulnerable God,
our Saviour.

Jeremiah 14:7-10,19-22
Psalm 84:1-7 Luke 18:9-14
2 Timothy 4:6-8,16-18

21 after Pentecost

The image of the helpless God may be a difficult one for some pray-ers. Yet the image of a naked and vulnerable Christ is common in many churches, and has been for centuries. In northern Europe about 1500 a type of image known as 'Christ on the cold stone' was carved; a full sized stone figure of Christ resting on the way to Calvary, usually with a cloth covering his loins and his hands bound with rope. One figure which featured in an exhibition at the National Gallery in London last year was unusual for its type because the figure of Christ was completely naked, wearing nothing but the crown of thorns. It is an image of Christ which shows total vulnerability as we see his exhaustion, his suffering. We can see this Christ in others around us or via the media; rejected refugees, exhausted asylum seekers, the victims of war and natural disaster from tiny babies to elderly people, those abandoned outside the benefit system, and all who are called 'socially excluded'. It is with this reality close to home that we can try to pray to the helpless God.

Janet Lees

Being vulnerable, being protective
What makes you feel vulnerable? In what circumstances do you feel helpless? In what ways do you respond to the vulnerability or helplessness of others? Collect together some of the things from your life which represent vulnerability and protection as a background to this prayer.

Pray with partner churches in Guyana.

123

Read: Luke 19:1-10

With his suit torn and his shoes scuffed
the superintendent of taxes
clambered down the tree
to welcome and be made welcome by
the one person he'd been longing to see.
It hadn't happened to him in years -
no-one welcomes a superintendent of taxes
unless they want something.

Well this man wanted something (though he didn't ask).
He wanted everything, in fact, everything times four,
not for himself, but for the poor
and the ones who had been cheated of their rights.
And in return he offered the one thing
that set the tax collector on his feet -
identity, community. Salvation came at last!

God whose care excludes no-one,
whose economy balances both rich and poor,
give us sensitivity to see the needs of all
and courage to speak your word of welcome
that enables others to welcome you.

22 after Pentecost

Tax collectors and sinners

When I first came to East Kilbride the huge office tower block that was Centre 1 dominated my horizon. From here the Inland Revenue taxed the workers of every Scottish based employer. The church was literally in its shadow. In the rest of Scotland, in popular humour, Centre 1 was "the enemy", and Scottish citizens fantasised about blowing the place up.

When I brought to East Kilbride my flippant throw-away remarks about tax collectors I met with much politeness, but no one fell about laughing in this town where everybody has a family member, friend or neighbour working for the Revenue. It had all the diplomatic success of telling mother-in-law jokes to mother-in-laws, or traffic warden jokes to the guy who is writing you a ticket. Tax Collectors in the New Testament seemed to operate on a franchise system from the Romans. They were collaborating with the occupying authorities, they were believed to feather their own nests and they were seen as parasitic of their own people. The tax collectors in Righead URC work to implement the decisions of the governments we elect. They try hard to behave justly towards the punters, and conscientiously towards the Revenue. Of course they are all a bunch of sinners - but I've learned that comes from being like the rest of us, not from being tax collectors.

Alan Paterson

Pray with **tax collectors.**

Holy God,
we thank you that you have chosen to be involved in our world,
rather than be some remote deity who controls life from afar.
Help us to remember our world today.

We grieve with you for the loss,
and injury to children, women and men
caught up in conflict throughout the world.
We remember all who have made sacrifices
so that we may live in peace and freedom,
just as you offered your Son
as the ultimate sacrifice for all people of every race and nation.

Help us in our remembering not to dwell on the past
but always look to the future.
May our remembering compel us to act
compassionately for victims of violence,
justly towards the perpetrators of conflict,
as peacebrokers with divided families and communities,
towards reconciliation in our own relationships.

Holy God,
help us to remember
and in remembering
commit ourselves to your shalom.

A time to remember

During the summer, members of an old people's day centre from the East End of London had a series of day trips. They chose to revisit the places where they or their children had been evacuated in the war. Most of the conversations on the journey focused on people's wartime experience. Although some lighthearted moments were recollected, for many there were stories of hardship and tragedy. A number of the people on the trips were Jewish, one part of the diverse nature of East London. What is more, Len, the volunteer who drove the minibus, not a church member as it happens, has a German wife; a fact Len anticipated most people would politely overlook and not allow to get in the way of their enjoyment of their day out.

As the minibus arrived back the minister was there to meet it. For two or three minute she asked people about the sort of memories which had been rekindled. She then invited people to be quiet as she said a few words of prayer...in all it took ten minutes.

Those ten minutes marked out the day centre's trip as different from what might be organized by a secular organisation. The words which were spoken and the thoughts and emotions which were evoked would otherwise have been hidden and isolating. As for Len with this German wife, he took away with him a sense of acceptance rather than avoidance. He saw how faith was not about denying reality but rather about looking at the facts of our humanity in all our vulnerability and destructiveness. I know this because Len told me about it, and he told his wife as well.

Ann Morisy

Pray with **peacemakers.**

Read: Isaiah 65:17-25

Creating God,
come quickly to this old world,
reshape and re-vision her
to be your new creation.

May poverty no longer be a barrier to good health care,
may everyone live in a home they call their own,
may the power of science be used to enrich communities.

Let joy and hope become marks of your church.
Recreate us as your partners in mission,
working with our neighbours,
so that the whole of creation shares in this new start.

Creating God,
come quickly to this old world,
reshape and re-vision her
to be your new creation.

24 after Pentecost

"....the past will no more be remembered"

The Loxley Valley, once the home of a number of small rolling mill companies, now lies silent. The mills have gone, the demolition contractors removed everything of value and have left the valley to its little river, its fish and birdlife. Similar happenings can be observed along the Five Weirs Walk, constructed through some of the old centres of Sheffield's steelworking. The water quality of the River Don is now sufficiently improved that it sustains fish and other aquatic life. Childhood dreams of fishing in the Don are now a reality, as also is being able to boat down Sheffield's canal without feeling that one was commuting along an open sewer. Improved water quality and the ability to sustain life may have been in the longer term achieved by legislation, but the prime mover in these environmental improvements has been the industrial desolation which has seen the river system change from amongst the most heavily polluted in the western hemisphere, into areas which with appropriate landscaping are truly pleasant and accessible for recreation.

Stewart Dalton

Pray with *scientists.*

Read: Luke 23:33-43

Voice 1   Is this the way to begin the new creation,
          a beloved son killed by occupying troops?
          Is this not rather the end – the end of life, hope and
          love?
          Where is the new start to be found?

Voice 2   The new start is found in the words of a criminal,
          words of recognition, words of hope for the future.
          'Jesus, remember me, when you come into your
          Kingdom'.

Voice 1   Crucified Christ,
          you experienced death
          so that we might have life in its fullest measure.
          Kindle within us that spark of life
          so we may be rejuvenated to live your Good News.

Voice 2   Risen Christ,
          you offer each of us a new start,
          an opportunity to take our place as
          children of God and citizens of your Kingdom.
          Give us courage to grasp that opportunity,
          and enable us to proclaim our faith with confidence.

Voice 1   Crucified and Risen Christ,
          King of the Jews and King of all peoples,
          come to live within our congregations
          that they may be witnesses to your reign,
          communities of life, hope and love,
          catalysts for renewal and a fresh start.

Jesus did not simply take upon himself a fate which he had to accept and endure. He left his Father's house of his own free will. It was his own decision to leave Galilee, where he undoubtedly had stronger support. In the end he went freely towards his own catastrophe, which we call the cross, no differently from thousands of organized workers, who could also lead a more peaceful and tranquil life at home.

Dorothy Solle

Christ carrying the cross, is not a tragic image, because carrying the cross - loving your neighbour - is daily work, like a window cleaner carrying his ladder, or whatever.

Neil MacGregor

You are sheltered by the grace of God;
You are accompanied by the Son of God;
You are renewed by the Spirit of God;
Take with you the Creator's grace, Christ's fellowship and the Spirit's energy:
these resources are yours, now and forever.

Janet Lees

Goodness is stronger than evil;
love is stronger than hate;
light is stronger than darkness;
life is stronger than death.
Victory is ours, victory is ours
through him who loved us.

Iona Community version of words by Desmond Tutu
The music is in There is one among us, Wild Goose Publications.

Pray with the staff of CWM and the regeneration of all our partner churches.

Contributors

The copyright of prayer material is held by the authors as follows:

Heather Pencavel for prayers dated
3rd December to 31st December
22nd April to 24th June
7th October to 4th November

Lindsey Sanderson for prayers dated
4th February to 1st April
1st July to 29th July
11th November to 25th November

Chris Warner for prayers dated
6th January to 28th January
8th April to 15th April
5th August to 30th September

Original photographs/illustrations by Leigh Jones on pages:
2, 43, 50, 58, 75, 102, 119, 123, 126, 129.

Acknowledgements

Christmas 1 - 31 December
Exchange in Sight, February 1999, EARAP

Epiphany - 6 January
both from 'Lookout' Winter 1999/2000, Industrial Mission in South Yorkshire. Used by permission

Epiphany 1 - 7 January
1 Linbert Spencer from *Wisdom is Calling* compiled by Geoffrey Duncan, published by the Canterbury Press. Used by permission
2 David Gamble is the Methodist Connexional Secretary for Family & Personal Relationships. From *Magnet*, No 48, Winter 1999, published by the Women's network of the Methodist Church. Used by permission

Epiphany 2 - 14 January
1 Derek Webster from *Wisdom is Calling* compiled by Geoffrey Duncan, published by the Canterbury Press. Used by permission
2 'You made a Difference', The Homelessness Sunday Prayer, written for the Scottish Churches Housing Agency

Epiphany 3 - 21 January
Children in Urban Regeneration, Community Development Journal, January 2000.
Used by permission

Epiphany 4 - 28 January
Dreams from Hard Places by Donnie Munro, published by Sabhal Mor Ostaig, Sleite, An t-Eilean Sgitheanach IV44 8RG. Used by permission

Epiphany 5 - 4 February
Christian Aid News, Winter 1999. Used by permission

Epiphany 6 - 11 February
CWM Inside Out, issue number 13, and Carys Humphries serving through CWM in Taiwan.
Used by permission

Epiphany 7 - 18 February
Both from Coracle, October 1999, published by the Iona Community

Epiphany 8 (Transfiguration) - 25 February
Speaking of God by Trevor Dennis (SPCK). Used by permission

Lent 1 - 4 March
1 *Stormy Seas We Brave: creative expressions of uprooted people.*
WCC Geneva 1998. Permission sought
2 Working with Family Diversity, DfEE Publications. Crown copyright is
reproduced with the permission of the Controller of Her Majesty's
Stationery Office

Lent 2 - 11 March
1 *Stormy Seas We Brave: creative expressions of uprooted people.*
WCC Geneva 1998. Permission sought
2 Christian Aid News, Spring 2000. Used by permission

Lent 3 - 18 March
Burngreave Messenger, Issue 2, December 1999

Lent 4 - 25 March
Both are reproduced with permission from John Brown Publishing who
publish 'Hotline' on behalf of Virgin Trains

Lent 5 - 1 April
A National Christian Response - The dispersal of asylum seekers under
the immigration and asylum act 1999. Practical Guide for Churches and
Church organisations. Churches' Commission for Racial Justice.
Used by permission

Palm Sunday - 8 April
Helen M Mee. Used by permission

Monday of Holy Week - 9 April
1 From a Theology of Flourishing for the next millennium, lecture given
for ACATE, September 1999 by Mary Grey
2 "A Women's Creed from Beijing", Catherine Keller, *Apocalypse Now
and Then: a feminist story of the end of the world.*
Boston: Beacon Press 1996. Used by permission

Tuesday of Holy Week - 10 April
Leaflet from Jim Cotter, 47 Firth Park Avenue, Sheffield S5 6HF

Good Friday - 13 April
1 'Lookout' Winter 1999/2000, Industrial Mission in South Yorkshire.
Used by permission
2 *Of Rolling Waters and Roaring Wind*, WCC Geneva 2000.
Permission sought

Easter Day - 15 April
from The Guardian, 'Face to Faith', Nicholas Jowett, 5.2.2000.
Used by permission

Easter 2 - 22 April
Beyond the Good Samaritan by Ann Morisy, Mowbray, an imprint of
Continuum. Used by permission

Easter 4 - 6 May
Walking on Water: Black American Lives at the turn of the 21st century
by Randall Kenan. Published by Little, Brown and Company, 1999.
Used by permission

Easter 5 Christian Aid Week - 13 May
The Vision of St Peter by Alan Payne
Source: BBC Radio Sheffield, Rony in the Morning : Write on with
Ray Hearne,
Tuesday 25 January 2000 : Knitting. Used by permission

Ascension - 24 May
Ascension Day by Chris Dolan 1999, published by Review, Headline
Books. Used by permission

Easter 7 - 27 May
from *Flame: The Methodist Magazine,* issue 1 © March/April 2000
Trustees for Methodist Church Purposes. Used by permission of the
publishers, Methodist Publishing House

Pentecost - 3 June
Of Rolling Waters and Roaring Wind, WCC Geneva 2000.
Permission sought

Trinity - 10 June
Skills for Neighbourhood Renewal: Local Solutions, DfEE Publications.
Crown copyright is reproduced with the permission of the Controller of
Her Majesty's Stationery Office

3 after Pentecost - 24 June
John L Bell, *States of Bliss and Yearning,* Wild Goose Publications, The Iona Community, Glasgow, 1998. Used by permission

4 after Pentecost - 1 July
RECYCLtd, Newsletter, 3 October 1999. Used by permission

5 after Pentecost - 8 July
Bromley By Bow Centre, Annual report 1995-6. Used by permission

6 after Pentecost - 15 July
Beyond the Good Samaritan by Ann Morisy, Mowbray, an imprint of Continuum. Used by permission

8 after Pentecost - 22 July
Peter Colwell (with apologies to Thomas Hardy) written on the 30th April 1999 following a bomb attack on the gay pub "The Admiral Duncan" in Soho, London. Used by permission

9 after Pentecost - 5 August
Skye and Lochalsh Enterprise Annual Report 1998/9. Used by permission

10 after Pentecost - 12 August
Coracle, Iona Community, April 1999. Used by permission

11 after Pentecost - 19 August
No Longer a Secret, WCC Geneva 1993. Permission sought

12 after Pentecost - 26 August
Masithandane Association, South Africa

13 after Pentecost - 2 September
Paul Skirrow, New Deal, a theological perspective. MitE (Mission in the Economy). Used by permission

14 after Pentecost - 9 September
1 Rosemary Varney, quoted in her obituary in the Guardian, 22.2.2000
2 Surprised by Joy in *Of Rolling Waters and Roaring Wind,* WCC Geneva. Permission sought

15 after Pentecost - 16 September
IMAgenda, February 2000. Used by permission

17 after Pentecost - 30 September
1 © Bob Warwicker, from *Dare to Dream* compiled by Geoffrey Duncan, published by Harper Collins. Used by permission
2 Paul Skirrow, New Deal, a theological perspective. MitE (Mission in the Economy). Used by permission

30 September
The Rich Christians and Poor Lazarus by Helmut Gollwitzer (translated by David Cairns), Saint Andrew Press 1970

18 after Pentecost - 7 October
Jaipur Limb Campaign News, December 1999. Used by permission

19 after Pentecost - 14 October
Skills for Neighbourhood Renewal: Local Solutions, DfEE Publications. Crown copyright is reproduced with the permission of the Controller of Her Majesty's Stationery Office

20 after Pentecost - 21 October
Four Faces of Scotland, The Scottish Review, May 1997. Used by permission

23 after Pentecost Remembrance Sunday - 11 November
Beyond the Good Samaritan by Ann Morisy, Mowbray, an imprint of Continuum. Used by permission

24 after Pentecost - 18 November
Crashing Steel by Stewart Dalton. ISBN: 1-871647-73-8. Price: £9.95. Wharncliffe Books, 47 Church Street, Barnsley, S Yorks S70 2BR. Used by permission

Last after Pentecost (Christ the King) - 25 November
1 *Choosing Life* by Dorothy Solle, Fortress Press 1981. Used by permission
2 An Advocate for Art, Third Way, March 2000
4 *An African Prayer Book* by Desmond Tutu. Reproduced by permission of Hodder & Stoughton Limited

COUNCIL FOR WORLD MISSION
MEMBER CHURCHES